Marla Taviano

From Blushing Bride to Wedded Wife

HARVEST HOUSE PUBLISHERS

EUGENE, OREGON

Cover by Garborg Design Works, Minneapolis, Minnesota

Back cover author photo © Camille Ackerman

FROM BLUSHING BRIDE TO WEDDED WIFE

Copyright © 2006 by Marla Taviano
Published by Harvest House Publishers
Eugene, Oregon 97402
www.harvesthousepublishers.com

Library of Congress Cataloging-in-Publication Data
Taviano, Marla, 1975-
    From blushing bride to wedded wife / Marla Taviano.
        p. cm.
    Includes bibliographical references.
    ISBN-13: 978-0-7369-1757-5 (pbk.)
    ISBN-10: 0-7369-1757-8 (pbk.)
    1. Wives—Biblical teaching. 2. Marriage—Biblical teaching. 3. Marriage—Religious aspects—Christianity. I. Title.
    BV4528.15.T38 2006
    248.8'435—dc22   2005025434

Printed in the United States of America

06 07 08 09 10 11 12 13 14 / VP-MS / 10 9 8 7 6 5 4 3 2 1

To Grandma Joan and Grandma Marilyn, two one-of-a-kind saints
who love words and books even more than I do.
You have both blessed my life immeasurably!

Contents

Let's Chat 7

Part I—Beginning the Journey
1. Great Expectations 13
2. The First Year 31

Part II—Loving Unselfishly
3. It's Not About Me 53
4. Fighting Fairly 77

Part III—Treating Hubby God's Way
5. Submission...Seriously? 101
6. R-E-S-P-E-C-T 119

Part IV—Cultivating Family Relationships
7. Family Matters 139
8. Your Hubby, Her Baby 159

Part V—Fanning the Flames
9. The Marriage Bed 183
10. Faithfulness in Action 203

Part VI—Building Your Home
11. That Woman from Proverbs 31 225
12. Where Is Your Treasure? 245

The Final Word 265
Notes 269

Let's Chat

I prayerfully considered waiting to write this book. Waiting until I was older, more experienced, more mature. Waiting until I'd mastered marriage—or at least gotten the hang of it. Then I wrote it anyway.

Sometimes all we need is someone we can relate to—not someone who has it all figured out. I don't claim to have all the answers. My marriage and I are both works in progress. I'm here to tell you that you're not alone. Marriage is tough, and nobody's perfect. Some people's just seem to be. I have a burden for freshly wedded wives, and I want God to speak through me straight to your heart.

I've read countless books on marriage written by older, godly women. Maybe you have too. Their insight gained from years of experience is invaluable. But on the flip side, when they speak of 25 years of marriage, perhaps you can't relate. You may not even be that old! Your silver anniversary is light-years away. Is there any hope for you in the near future?

My situation is a little less imposing and easier to imagine. "She's been married six years," you say. "That's just 2000 days away. I've already come 12!"

If you're looking for a perfect marriage to model yours after, you've come to the wrong book. But if you want to know how to bounce back after screwing up, I'm your girl!

In his bestselling book *The Purpose-Driven Life*, Rick Warren shares an exciting truth. "People are more encouraged when we share how God's grace helped us in weakness than when we brag about our strengths."[1]

He also writes, "While it is wise to learn from experience, it is *wiser* to learn from the experiences of others. There isn't enough time to learn everything in life by trial and error. We must learn from the life lessons of one another."[2]

Take good notes on my marital mess ups, and you'll save yourself a few years of grief!

What Kind of Book *Is* This?

This is a sit-back-and-relax-with-a-bowl-of-chips kind of book. Or a cup of cappuccino. Or an apple and a bottled water. Whatever makes you happy.

Originally, I envisioned a devotional with end-of-the-chapter Scripture passages to study, sample prayers to pray, and practical activities to incorporate into your marriage.

Then I chucked it all. I was in the middle of another marriage book that had all those things, and—call me shallow—I either skimmed through them or skipped over them. I was in a hurry to get to the juicier parts of the book.

In the busyness of my day, reading time is a precious commodity, and I want it to be relaxing. I study my Bible each morning and don't feel like looking up verses during my "fun" reading time—as unspiritual as that sounds.

This isn't a workbook, and it's not for your husband to read with you. It's for you—designed to bring a smile to your lips and encouragement to your heart. That little boost you need to get to work on making your marriage honoring to God and your husband—and worth every minute you invest in it.

In this book, I tell it like it is. There's no beating around the bush.

Nothing is off-limits. It's honest, real, practical, and straightforward. I know you're hungry for the truth—none of this watered-down stuff—and I'm going to feed it to you.

I want this book to be comforting, relaxing, and enticing. I want each sentence, paragraph, and chapter to grab your attention and keep you reading. Instead of begging you not to skip the boring parts, I'll just leave them out!

However, this does not mean that the whole book is wildly entertaining, without any Scripture verses or spiritual insights—there are many. There's just no homework at the end of each chapter or a million ideas you'll never use.

Most of the chapters in this book are geared toward newlyweds, but married women of any age can benefit from these truths. Some I've just recently learned to apply to my own marriage. I'm no expert yet, but I didn't want to wait to pass them on!

My prayer is that, as you read this book, you will be like the Bereans whom Luke commended in Acts 17:11. "Now the Bereans were of more noble character than the Thessalonians, for they received the message with great eagerness and examined the Scriptures every day to see if what Paul said was true."

Don't take my word for it! If I give you advice that you aren't sure is biblical, check it out for yourself in God's Word.

A Biblical Worldview

No doubt you've already picked up on the fact that this book approaches marriage from a Christian worldview. This comes as no surprise if you picked up this book at a Christian bookstore.

If you didn't, please accept my heartfelt thanks for not putting the book down by this point—or throwing it in the trash. Maybe you were searching for a book about marriage on the Internet, and the cover of this one caught your eye.

You had no idea it was going to be a book based on the Bible, with old-fashioned, outdated—even ridiculous—ideas about marriage. When you perused the table of contents and saw the word "submission," you probably fought the urge to send the book back and demand a refund.

I have a favor to ask, my friend—a two-parter. First of all, I ask you to hear me out. Read the book from cover to cover with an open mind.

Then, go back to your marriage and try things *your* way, the world's way, the twenty-first-century way. If that works, and your marriage blossoms, and your heart is filled with joy and peace and fulfillment—awesome.

But if by some chance your marriage still leaves something to be desired, promise me you'll retrieve this book from the box in the basement and give my ideas—God's ideas, actually—another thought. Will you do that for me? For *you?*

Let the Journey Begin!

Let's pretend this isn't just a book but a heart-to-heart chat. We'll be two old friends sitting on the sofa, catching up with each other and sharing how marriage is treating us. We'll be candid and open with each other as only girlfriends can be. We'll laugh a lot and learn something too. Come and sit down! I saved you a seat! Oh, this is going to be fun!

Part One

Beginning the Journey

1

Great Expectations

May the God of hope
fill you with all joy and peace
as you trust in him,
so that you may overflow with hope
by the power of the Holy Spirit.

Romans 15:13

Let's get real here. Is your marriage all you dreamed it would be and more? Are your days and nights filled with adoring gazes, flying sparks, terms of endearment, and passionate lovemaking? Have all the cares and worries of life melted into oblivion?

As you consider your answer, you have two options—affirmative or negative. Yes, all of the above is true. Or no, my marriage is not as great as all that. In other words, you can lie, or you can tell the truth.

How did this happen? How did you go from blushingly beautiful bride to woefully wedded wife in such short time? Mere months ago, you were standing there in all your bridal glory, on the cusp of that glorious dream called marriage. You remember it like it was yesterday…

Bye-Bye, Blushing Bride!

The long-awaited wedding day. You've dreamed about it, planned for it, stressed over it—and it's finally here! Today is your day! You're getting married!

The morning passes by in a blur. Your hair is done, your makeup perfect, your friends and sisters giggling as they slip into matching dresses.

You want to relish each moment, but they all pass so quickly. You try to soak up each precious second to relive later, but you're in a trance. You pinch yourself as you gaze into the mirror. Am I actually here? Is that beauty in white truly me? Am I really about to become his wife?

The walk down the aisle on Daddy's arm goes by too fast. The vows are over before you can blink. The pronouncement. The kiss. The cake. The dancing. The hugs. The food. The pictures. The smiles. The small talk with friends, relatives, strangers. Nodding, smiling, not hearing a word they say. Tossing your bouquet.

Ever in your dreamlike state, you dodge the birdseed, climb in the car, tuck in your billowing gown, and off you go, waving and honking, cans rattling behind you.

Then it's your wedding night. The honeymoon you've dreamed about for years. Then it too is over.

Now you're home. The home you now share with your husband. You're married. *Married!* Time begins to slow back down. Reality sets in—and you panic.

Am I ready for this? Am I prepared to be this man's wife? Aaahh— I'm a *wife!* I have a *husband!* I don't know if I can go through with this!

You're in shock. You have a new last name. You live in a new town or state. Your role in life is a completely new one. You're beginning to realize what a huge responsibility that is. The identity crisis begins.

You burn your first supper. You have no clue how to change the batteries in the smoke alarm. Your husband steals your covers and passes more gas than any human should. He leaves the toilet seat up, his smelly underwear on the floor, and his whiskers all over the bathroom sink.

Sex is nothing like you fantasized it would be. In fact, nothing is. You've already had your first fight, and it was a big one. You're arguing over where to spend Christmas—six months from now!

You're lonely, confused, and scared to death. Being a newlywed wasn't supposed to be like this! Every romantic notion you've ever had—all your hopes and dreams for your marriage—dashed!

All around you are people who have it all together. They're living the dream that has somehow eluded you. Their marriages are perfect. Yours is a disaster. And you've only been married 27 days!

Marriage was supposed to be like dating but better. The only differences were to be wonderful ones, like living and sleeping together. Everything would be easier, more exciting. You expected your life together to be nothing short of charming. Paradise. A constant state of warm, fuzzy, dreamy ecstasy.

So where are all those feelings, and why do you feel like bawling your eyes out? Where did you go wrong? Why are you such a failure? Are you the only one in the world who feels this way?

Shhh…calm down…it's going to be okay. Just sit down for a moment and relax. Take a deep breath. In. And out. And know that you are not alone! Countless other women understand *exactly* how you feel. Let that encourage you as you embark on this journey called marriage.

The Honeymoon

What better way to start that journey than with a honeymoon—a word packed full of romantic connotations. Yet for some of us, the honeymoon wasn't all it was cracked up to be.

My cousin Camy began hers in tears, sobbing because she couldn't wear her fabulous wedding dress on the plane. "I don't want to take it off already!" she cried. "It all went by too fast!"

I wasn't as attached to my bridal finery. I had sucked my stomach in long enough for one day. My comfy track pants and favorite sweatshirt were like a soothing balm to my body. I kept my curls in place, though, leaving the pound of birdseed embedded in my updo undisturbed.

As we drove along that never-ending highway, my stomach somersaulted like a gymnast on caffeine pills. This was finally it. In a matter of hours, I would see my husband naked—and we'd be having sex. Panic set in.

Was there any way to rewind time to allow me to get used to the whole idea? I'd been waiting for this day since puberty. Dreaming about it daily—and nightly—for the past six months. Why was I chickening out now?

Spending ten days in a secluded mountain cabin in January sounded perfect *before* I got married. No people. No distractions. Just lots of hot, steamy sex. I hadn't taken into consideration the fact that it might hurt. By day two, I would have given anything for a Get Out of Sex Free card, but my husband wasn't passing them out.

You're not alone if your first sexual experience with your husband was a far cry from the hot and heavy thrill ride you'd been mentally picturing for months. On a scale of one to ten, most people (if they're honest) would give their wedding night a three or four.

I hadn't considered the possibility that sex might last ten whole minutes on average. I didn't realize we would max out at three times in one day (which hasn't happened since). Who knew that the two hours of making out we did when we were dating would be replaced by a handful of minutes in bed?

What were we supposed to do with ourselves the *rest* of the day?

We had two options—hiking or watching a movie. Both got old quickly. I didn't expect to be *bored* on my honeymoon!

I didn't expect to be sick either. I came down with the flu on our wedding night, fought a fever for three days, and threw up in the Burger King bathroom sink (didn't quite make it to the toilet). And the hiking was enough to kill me—if I didn't die from the pain of sex first.

Let's face it. A wedding isn't the most ideal way to start a marriage. I'm not the only bride to endure the strain of planning a wedding—the pressure of demands and deadlines, the sleepless hours, the emotional roller coaster—only to collapse on my wedding night with a fever and chills. Our bodies can only take so much.

Being with someone else 24/7 was hard for me to get used to. I took my privacy for granted until it was gone. At times I just wanted to get away—far, far away—and curl up with a good book for a few hours.

I remember one instance in particular when all my heart desired was one little ten-minute shower...alone.

Our honeymoon cabin had a roomy two-person Jacuzzi tub and a cramped one-half person shower. I'm a bit claustrophobic as it is, especially if the tight place gets hot and steamy.

My husband was under the impression that married couples (if they really love each other) shower together whenever possible. So, five or six times on our honeymoon, we packed our bodies like sardines into that phone-booth shower and attempted to wash ourselves before I ran out of oxygen.

As soon as I rinsed the last drop of conditioner out of my hair, I would fling open the door, rush out of the bathroom, and drink in huge gulps of air, while Gabe lingered in the steamy sauna another 15 minutes.

At first, he took my quick exit as a personal affront, but he soon concluded that I couldn't help my aversion to cramped, hot quarters. These days, we shower together about once a year, and then only until I hyperventilate.

Our photos from our honeymoon show us happy, in love, and having the time of our lives. And I'm sure there were some lovely moments. But since the premise of this book is candidness, let me summarize the honeymoon our camera failed to capture.

It was boring and disappointing, I was sick half the time, sex hurt, taking a simple shower was a nightmare, and we spent much more money than we could afford. They say that once the honeymoon ends, reality will immediately set in. I didn't have to wait that long.

Lessons in a Laundromat

I remember one Friday night just two months into our less-than-glamorous marriage. While the rest of the world was out partying, I was in the Laundromat, waiting for the rinse cycle.

In years past, weekends were all about food, fun, friends, and football. Friday nights as a newlywed meant sitting home alone while Gabe worked.

This is as bad as it gets, I thought. I'm all alone on a Friday night in the Laundromat, of all places. I can't afford a washer and dryer because I'm a substitute teacher and my husband is still in college. Even if I *could* afford them, they wouldn't fit in our cramped apartment.

I'm sick of eating frozen pizzas and not being able to buy anything fun. I have no friends. I'm lonely, bored, and depressed. I think God has forsaken me.

As my clothes were spinning and rinsing, my eyes swelled with tears. In theory (and in hindsight), life as newlyweds was a beautiful thing, but as we struggled to pay the bills, get through school, start careers, and find our way in the world, I couldn't see the beauty of it.

I was searching for some tangible kind of happiness. Something beyond washing dishes and making the bed, more noble than picking up Gabe's dirty clothes or fixing his supper. Opening our new appliances and wedding gifts had been fun, but the newness had worn off weeks ago. Was this all there was to life?

What's Left to Look Forward To?

We women tend to get caught up in the "anticipation" phenomenon. We love to plan and dream, but when The Big Day finally comes, it ends with somewhat of a letdown.

Think of Christmas. There's so much excitement leading up to it, but when you open up your presents and it's all over…bummer.

Or a family vacation. I remember being so excited about a big trip when I was younger, even packing my clothes days in advance. Then it came. And went. Another letdown.

Everything seems so rosy when you're engaged—because you always have something to look forward to. The feelings you have as you talk and dream and kiss are perfectly magical. And we assume they'll continue after marriage.

"I thought we could just cuddle and gaze into each other's eyes all the time," my friend Janet told me. But it often ends up being more like December twenty-sixth, or coming home from the beach. With nothing left to look forward to, our dreamy ideas about marriage bite the dust.

When we dream, we leave out all the not-so-great parts—like stinky feet and uncooperative husbands. Who dreams about living on a shoestring budget and fighting about each other's mother? Or annoying mannerisms? Or sex that ends with him in a huff and you in tears?

In reality, married love is different from dating love. Dating love is stimulating, titillating, fluttering, and electrifying. It flirts with the element of the unknown. The relationship lives and breathes on the brink of disaster. At any given moment, one of you could decide you want out, and boom—it's all over.

With marriage comes stability and predictability. Booooring.

Dating Love vs. Married Love

"Most of us enter marriage by way of the 'in love' experience," Gary Chapman says. We meet someone whose physical traits and personality create "enough electric shock to trigger our 'love alert' system." That tingly feeling keeps getting stronger. This person is The One.

"At its peak, the 'in love' experience is euphoric," Chapman continues. "We are emotionally obsessed with each other. We long to be together…we believe…we will always have the wonderful feelings that we have at this moment."[1]

Studies show that the average life span of this romantic obsession is two years. The euphoria of the "in love" experience gives us the illusion of intimacy and complete unselfishness toward each other. "I'd do absolutely anything for you!" we say.

Then reality hits, and we realize how egocentric we really are. Sure, we'll do anything for this person—as long as it's what *we* want, and *he* reciprocates.

When the euphoria starts to fade, we think we have fallen out of love. The reality is that it wasn't real love to begin with. Love is not something you fall in and out of—it's a conscious choice you make to treat someone a certain way. You *did* fall, but it wasn't into *love*. And you *will* fall out as everyone eventually does. The question of the hour is this: What will you do when those feelings of infatuation go away?

This is what separates the women from the girls. Will you dump your marriage and search for someone else who will make you feel that emotional high again? Or will you suck it up and pursue *real* love with your spouse? A lot of divorces today boil down to nothing more than "I've lost that lovin' feelin'."

Gary Thomas writes, "The idea that a marriage can survive on romance alone...has wrecked many a marital ship. Romantic love has no elasticity to it. It can never be stretched; it simply shatters. Mature love, the kind demanded of a good marriage, must stretch."[2]

If we crave that romantic love so much, we should just date guy after guy and forget marriage. Unless of course we're Christians who believe sex outside of marriage is wrong. Then we'd have to be celibate our whole lives.

Besides that, we want to have our cake and eat it too. We want the familiarity of marriage *and* the excitement of dating—a combination that can't be consistently maintained day in and day out for years on end.

"The romantic roller coaster of courtship eventually evens out to the terrain of a Midwest interstate—long, flat stretches with an occasional overpass," Thomas writes.[3]

As time goes on, hopefully we'll realize that we kind of *like* the terrain of the Midwest highway—and nice little hills *do* pop up here and there. Sometimes even thrilling mountains.

As most people soon realize, the dating game isn't all it's cracked up to be. The euphoria is great, sure, but it doesn't last, and it lacks deeper meaning. We love adventure and excitement, but familiarity and comfort can be a welcome change of pace.

Puzzle Trouble

I was sitting at the kitchen table, scowling as I put together a 500-piece puzzle. It was a Valentine's Day present for Gabe—an excuse

to spend more time with my new husband. I was putting it together
alone.

Excitement and adventure? Ha! I was willing to settle for familiarity and comfort. Anything was better than loneliness. Gabe was in the
study, fiddling with a new computer program, and I was fighting off
feelings of hurt and rejection.

Helen Rowland once said that "when a girl marries, she exchanges
the attentions of all the other men of her acquaintance for the in-
attention of just one." Amen, sister.

I took pride in Gabe's computer savvy, but in those early days of
marriage, I felt as if I were competing for his attention with a machine
much smarter and more exciting than I was.

This wasn't how I had envisioned the whole marriage scenario.
Gabe was supposed to be captivated by me at all times.

"I can't get enough of you," he should be saying. Instead, he forgot
I even existed.

"This puzzle is pretty hard," I said out loud. To myself.

I raised my voice a notch. "I'll *never* be able to finish it."

Another notch. "And it doesn't look like I can count on any help
from my *hubby.*"

I had hoped Gabe would overhear and come running, apologizing
profusely for neglecting me. He didn't.

My, I was a champ at feeling sorry for myself. One tiny move from
Gabe, intentional or not, triggered my self-pity into action. It didn't
even have to be something he *did.* It could have been something I
thought he should have known to do and *didn't.* It was obvious to me
and should have been to him. Isn't that logical?

Your Husband, the Mind Reader

We girls go into marriage with elaborate mental images of how it should be run, and we truly expect that everything will go as planned. Yet this theory has a few kinks.

For one thing, we forgot to inform our husbands of The Plan. We just assumed they knew—that they could read our minds. They don't. They can't.

Maybe you're one of those who *did* inform her husband of The Plan—in laborious detail. Perhaps you even typed it up for him, specifying his particular role in each aspect of your marriage. Maybe you highlighted what his reactions and responses should be to any number of marital circumstances.

If so, your problems are of another variety and won't be adequately addressed in this book.

My friend Jodie comments on the biggest problem she has had to overcome in her marriage. "Sometimes I don't say what I'm thinking," she says, "yet I expect Jason to understand. He has no earthly idea that I'm upset or disappointed. I've learned that I have to verbalize how I feel."

Another friend echoed Jodie's sentiments. "I wish I would have known that husbands can not have a clue that something is bothering you, let alone know what it is."

My mom, married more than 30 years, often tells me, "Never expect your husband to read your mind! Always tell him how you feel!"

What if we know all that, but we still think that life would be a whole lot better if our husbands could read our minds? It just seems right. Men are supposed to know what we're thinking. I mean, really, it just ruins things when we have to actually come out and *tell* them. How unromantic!

Karen Scalf Linamen jokes that when it comes to romance, "our husbands would do well to don swami turbans and read crystal balls. They might as well, you know, because it is certainly unreasonable to expect us to make things easy for them by actually *verbalizing* the things that we want and need."[4]

Misguided Expectations

Mind reading isn't the only unrealistic—and unfair—expectation we have concerning our husbands and marriage. We've subconsciously compiled a long list of expectations in our minds and get upset when hubby doesn't live up to them. But if we fail to make our lists reasonable and realistic, we'll never be content with life as we know it—as it really is.

One big misconception we have is that since we love each other, all this marriage stuff is going to be a breeze. How could it not be, what with all the floating on the clouds and the incredible sex and all that?

One young wife told me, "I thought the wedding was the end result of our relationship, rather than the beginning. I thought we'd absolutely love every minute together."

When we walk down the aisle, we aren't thinking about how much hard work marriage is going to take. We assume it will come naturally, but actually there is a natural drift *apart,* and we have to fight to maintain oneness. Try telling that to a couple in the throes of a passionate dating relationship. Marriage hard work? Are you kidding?

Then there's the simple truth that we don't have a clue. We can't possibly understand marriage completely until we've lived it. Yet somehow we think we have grasped and mastered the concept before we even say "I do." Who are we fooling?

How many of us thought our husbands were nearly perfect—until we married them? "Sure, he has a cute habit or two that could get annoying," you mused, "but he'll probably outgrow them once we're married."

If only I had a dollar for every engaged woman who thinks those words to herself and then has to *eat* them after she gets married.

While dating, you put your best face forward, eagerly presenting yourself in the most positive light. You proudly display your strengths and carefully tuck away your weaknesses.

Once you're married, watch out! The love of your life now sees you as you really are. You can't take the strain of showing your best side all the time. You let down your guard. You allow your spouse to see the not-so-great qualities in your character he never realized were there. And you see all of his. Marriage—the unfriendly microscope.

Selfish Expectations

Be honest. In your vivid and vibrant daydreams of married life, did you picture all that you would *give* to your marriage or all that you would *get* out of it?

I'll admit most of my dreams were selfish ones. I didn't get married because I was just dying to serve my husband and spend my days meeting his needs. I was all about my own fulfillment and happiness.

"When I get married," I thought, "my husband will rub *my* back, massage *my* feet, run his fingers through *my* hair. When I get married, people will look at *me*, respect *me*, be envious of *me*. When people see the wedding ring on *my* finger, it will symbolize that *I* am attractive, wanted, taken. I'll have someone to love *me*, take care of *me*, affirm *me*. I'll have everything *I've* ever wanted."

A woman gets married expecting that her new husband will meet all of her needs—the need for security, affection, self-worth, and intimacy for starters. Even if you think of yourself as a modern married woman who doesn't need a man, deep down inside, we were all created with those longings.

What happens when hubby doesn't satisfy those longings? Disappointment, hurt, bitterness, and anger follow.

You're right to think that your husband is the one person on earth who can meet the biggest percentage of your needs, but he can't meet them all. God created us with a void in our hearts and lives that only He can fill. Your Creator is the only one who can complete you.

Whether or not we realize or admit it, we all crave intimacy with God. When we have that intimacy, we don't make such unrealistic demands on our spouses, and our marriages thrive.

I'm still learning these truths, and it's not easy. When I stop looking to Gabe to meet all my needs, I free him to meet the ones God created him to meet.

The Perfect Family

When we were little, my cousins Kyla and Kelly and I spent hours and hours making family photo albums. We cut out pictures of catalog models to represent the families we hoped to have someday. We glued the pictures onto notebook paper and named our husbands and children, writing commentaries beside each one.

I was always 26 years old in my family album. I suppose that was the perfect age. Young and vivacious yet old enough to have two or three kids if I got off to an early start.

I passed the 26-year-old mark a couple years ago, so I'm living out that photo album now. The funny thing is that some things about my life just don't match up. According to the album, by age 26, my husband "Nick" (27) and I were supposed to have four gorgeous, well-behaved children, all ten months apart.

I was supposed to have a Barbie-doll figure (complete with the perky C-cups), long, luscious, naturally blond hair, impeccable makeup, and a gorgeous but healthy tan. No stretch marks or saggy parts in sight.

"Nick" was supposed to be tall, dark, and handsome, with pearly white teeth, wavy hair, and muscles bulging out of his polo shirt. Sadly, Gabe looks more like "Nick" than I look like the Marla I imagined.

My hobbies, according to my predictions long ago, should include photography, gardening, and running in marathons.

"Nick" should be spending his free time cleaning the bathroom, playing with our children, and adoring his wife.

Well, I do enjoy taking pictures, and I would love to have a garden someday. And I ran cross-country in high school, but my running endeavors of late have been sporadic at best.

Gabe does adore me (in a more reserved way than I'm sure I'd imagined) and spends time with our children, but I don't think he would consider those his hobbies. As for cleaning the bathroom, he did help me scrub the tub *once* way back in our second year of marriage.

I know a few girls who are still clinging to those dreams of yesteryear. One friend of mine insists she will have five children in five years—all the while maintaining her current hobbies, slender figure, and impeccable style.

If your aspirations are as lofty as hers, I will hold my tongue, and your bubble will remain intact—for now. Come back when you have a few more years of marriage and a couple kids under your belt, and we'll talk.

Monopoly Money

As I grew older, my dream didn't change much. The ideals of a handsome, loving husband, beautiful children, a home, and even a career stood firm. I added some choice details as I reached puberty— the romance, cuddling, kissing. I left out a few details—the ones not glamorous enough for daydreams. But even shopping for groceries together sounded romantic to me.

As it turned out, our first trip to the grocery as married people wasn't very romantic.

Initially, it was fun to go down the aisles with Gabe and put things in our cart. I was six years old again playing house, filling my miniature orange and yellow plastic cart with tiny cereal boxes and plastic soup cans and paying with monopoly money. Oh, to have back the days when we could pay the bills with board-game currency!

I made a grocery list I thought was all-inclusive. Yet I bought more items that *weren't* on my list than *were* on it. It added up so quickly. Who would have guessed the ingredients for a simple casserole would cost so much? My dreams of being a world-class cook—adored by my husband and admired by our guests—were quickly coming to an end. Frozen pizzas were by far the easiest and cheapest meals I could buy.

Not to mention the fact that Gabe and I had vastly different tastes. We couldn't agree on beverages, ice cream flavors, brands of cereal, snacks, or even bread. White? Wheat? Rye? What about veggies? Fresh? Frozen? Canned? (Or Gabe's choice—none at all.) What a dilemma.

The sizeable difference between fantasy and reality was shocking.

But I Thought...

Author Joanne Heim shares some of her unmet expectations for marriage. "I would magically become as beautiful as I'd always dreamed of being," she says, "instantly know how to cook gourmet meals and leave all my problems behind...I really thought marriage would turn me into a new and improved version of me."

She goes on to say, "Our [wedding] plans came together perfectly, and I assumed that our marriage would come off equally well. Never mind that we made a lot of wedding plans but not very many marriage plans."[5]

I handed out a survey to every married woman I know, and as I read through the answers, I had to laugh at some of their unrealistic expectations for married life.

"I thought he would pick up after himself."

"I expected to make our home more of a refuge for my husband."

"I thought our sex life would be more in sync."

"I expected him to be as romantic as he had been while we were dating."

"I thought we'd be able to make it just like we had read in our marriage books."

"I expected unconditional love and freedom to be me."

"I thought he would help me clean the house without me asking him to."

"I expected him to become a Christian."

"I thought he would want to be with me all the time."

"I thought everything in life would be easier, but work is still hard."

"I expected him to be more of an initiator."

"I thought that he had paid off his credit card debt, but he hadn't."

"I thought my husband would be all I'd need, but I miss my family."

"I thought he would find every special day in our history worth celebrating."

"I thought we would both still be close with our single friends."

"I thought I would want sex more."

If you're not married yet, you may still be holding on for dear life to some of these same expectations. If you're already a newlywed, you know what these women are talking about! Isn't it great to know you're not alone?

I've tried to strike a balance in this book. On one hand, I want to give you practical tips and biblical principles that will help you improve yourself and your marriage. Insights and strategies that will convict you and help you make changes in your heart and life.

On the other hand, sometimes we just need to know that someone else understands. We need someone to let us know she gets it, that she's been there.

So you'll get nice heaping helpings of advice and principles. But you'll also get plenty of appetizers and side dishes of "I feel your pain."

Pull up a chair, put on your bib (this could get messy!), hand me your plate, and I'll start piling on the grub!

The First Year

If a man has recently married…
for one year he is to be free
to stay at home and bring happiness
to the wife he has married.

DEUTERONOMY 24:5

As a college student, I spent three months teaching in Japan. I prepared as best I could but still experienced culture shock upon arrival. Japan was not America. Everything seemed different—the money, the people, the food, everything. I knew a total of five words in Japanese. Living in Japan would be an adjustment.

Getting married is like moving to a foreign country. You will experience some culture shock. You and your husband won't always speak the same language. Living in marriage will be an adjustment.

Your first year of married life might be one of the most difficult you'll ever face. Take your time and allow yourself (and your husband) to adjust to your new "culture." In time, the shock will wear off, and you'll begin to feel at home. You'll even forget what life was like in your "old country"!

That's great, you say, but I'm not moving overseas. I'm just getting married—what's the big deal?

I'm glad you asked. Marriage is much more complex than we realize when we're dating.

"Even though we knew each other since kindergarten," my friend Patty says, "we didn't really know each other until after we got married. It was an exciting, surprising, bumpy time."

Those First Few Months

I asked women to describe how they felt during their first few months of wedded wifehood. The response was a wide spectrum of emotional adjectives—overwhelmed, scared, lonely, frustrated, content, inept, irritated, determined, confused, excited, disillusioned, happy, grateful, disappointed, trapped, angry, and maybe even self-righteous.

Some of the women I surveyed had glowing reports of their post-honeymoon lives. I believe them (for the most part), but I know that our memories tend to be selective—especially as time goes on.

> "Marital bliss! I loved it! We had a blast at everything!"

> "It was wonderful to finally be together so much."

> "Our first few months were great. We really didn't argue about anything."

> "It was very hard to go back to work after our honeymoon."

> "I thought I was dreaming and he'd have to go home."

> "We were passionate lovers. We enjoyed being constant companions."

When I asked women to go into detail about those first few months, the word "adjustment" came up a lot.

> "There was that weird, tough adjustment period that you sometimes hear of."

> "Learning to live day in and day out with someone who

was raised with different habits, morals, and rules—that was an adjustment."

"There were lots of adjustments because we were opposite in personality."

"The hardest adjustment for me has been staying up until 2:00 AM. My husband would rather sleep in than go to bed early."

"It was a time of adjustment. Instead of just doing what I wanted when I wanted, there was now another person to consider."

Did you catch the verse at the beginning of the chapter? Try reading it to your husband. "According to the Bible," you tell him, "for one year, you're supposed to devote every waking hour to my happiness."

Brace yourself for a laugh and adjust to the fact that it's not gonna happen.

The Fear Factor

Many women expressed that getting married was also a fearful experience—at least initially.

"I was scared I wouldn't be a good wife!" my friend Rachel admitted.

"We were so worried that we wouldn't be able to survive financially," my friend Mary Ann told me.

"I couldn't cook!" Gabe's aunt Chris says, laughing. "Believe it or not, that was the main thing that worried me because Jim likes to eat!"

My friend Pat said that getting married was "frightening because I left everything I knew—my family, home, and job—to move to a new state and a military lifestyle."

Other women commented that they were afraid they couldn't be the wives their husbands needed or wanted. The good news? Your hubby doesn't *know* what he needs or wants. You can learn and grow together. We shouldn't underestimate the work involved, but panicking doesn't do any good.

One woman told me that it helps to "realize that this first year is a transition time and not the permanent state of your relationship." Well said.

Getting in the Groove

I don't remember how long it took after my wedding for me to feel like I was really married and not just playing house. I'm sure it was many months, if not years. Even now, months away from turning 30, I don't always feel grown-up enough to be a wife, let alone a mom.

It can take a while to get used to everything new in your life—new husband, new name, new driver's license, new bank account, new Social Security card, new address, new phone number, new signature, new title—and that's just the beginning.

I visited my sister this summer, a couple weeks after her wedding. Her little apartment brought back memories of my own first home.

Sets of sheets—still in the package—stacked in her bedroom closet, mismatched furniture—Mom and Dad's castoffs—in the living room, the freezer stocked with Totino's "combination" party pizzas. A sparkling new coffeemaker, can opener, and toaster. A pile of wedding gifts to return, a stack of partially written thank-you notes, a spare bedroom decorated with a hodgepodge of everything that didn't match the rest of the décor. Ahhh...the memories.

Our first apartment was a total throwback—straight out of the '70s—with dark wood-paneled walls in the living room, mustard yellow and olive green wallpaper in the kitchen, gray paneling in both bedrooms, brown shag carpet, and mustard-colored sink, toilet, tub, and linoleum. It was even lovelier than it sounds.

Our couches cost $50 for the pair—and looked it. Our kitchen table was a steal at $40—with four wobbly chairs thrown in the deal. Our bed and dresser were $100 together—and actually quite beautiful. Our end tables and lamps were $5 and $10—castoffs from a funeral home. And we each contributed some furniture from our parents' homes.

I proudly displayed my new kitchen appliances. Even if I never once used my wok, my cappuccino maker, or my electric knife, just owning them made me feel like a real cook, a real wife.

Whether you moved straight from your parents' home to the home you now share with your husband, or you've lived as a single gal for years and years, adjusting to being married takes time.

So if you wake up some days completely unable to wrap your mind around the fact that you are a married woman with your very own home and your very own husband, never fear. You're quite normal.

You're Not Alone

You are not alone. Aren't those heartening words? We often think no one understands what we're going through, but that's not true. No problem we face or sin we struggle with is unique.

I had been feeling discouraged—all alone—my first Christmas as a married woman. When a holiday newsletter arrived in the mail, God knew it was just what I needed to lift my spirits. My friend J.J. had gotten married in May, and I hadn't seen her since. Reading between the lines of her letter, I felt as if I were at a support group for newlyweds and found a kindred spirit. The parallels in our lives seemed uncanny.

"It is exam time for Andy, so I have been delegated the honorable job of writing our very first Christmas letter." Just change "Andy" to "Gabe," and I could use this very sentence!

"Though small, our current residence is much larger than the shoebox-size apartment we lived in during the summer." Gabe and I also lived in a barely-bigger-than-a-shoebox apartment.

"Married life has been wonderful. My varied schedule leaves Andy eating microwave meals frequently, but I try to keep the house as tidy as possible (much cleaner than his bachelor pad last year!)." I couldn't have said it better myself.

"I turned 23 in November, so I'm starting to feel old." And I had turned 23 in October and felt ancient.

"Finding a church we like has been tricky, but we have settled on one for a few months now and hope to become more involved." Again, same.

I took this letter as a sign from God that He never meant for His children to face anything alone. In His grace, He brings people into our lives who are walking in our very shoes.

I love Romans 15:5-6. "May the God who gives endurance and encouragement give you a spirit of unity among yourselves as you follow Christ Jesus, so that with one heart and mouth you may glorify the God and Father of our Lord Jesus Christ."

Praise God for the spirit of unity among newly married women.

No One Warned Me!

My friend Abigail gave birth to her first child two weeks ago. "How are you feeling?" I asked her last night on the phone.

"Better now," she said. "But I felt awful the first few days after I got home. Why didn't anyone tell me I would feel so awful?"

I smiled to myself and offered kind words of empathy.

Wouldn't it be nice if someone could tell us how things are going to be each time we enter a new situation in life? Like marriage. "Why didn't anyone tell me it was going to be like this?" you wonder.

If you're reading this book before you get married, congratulations! You have your very own resource to tell you how marriage is going to be! Every marriage is different, yes, but you'd be surprised at how much we all share in common.

There's truly nothing new under the sun. What you're going through isn't news to anyone. And chances are if it's an I-just-got-married-and-I'm-clueless sort of thing, then thousands of women are experiencing the same thing as we speak.

Come laugh with me as you listen to some of my friends share what they wish someone had warned them about before they tied the knot.

> "That men somehow cannot see the little whisker pieces they leave all over after they shave. Even when you show them, they'll still swear they cleaned the sink."

> "How much my husband would remind me that 'your body is not your own' is a biblical statement (even if he uses it out of context)."

> "That men are a lot like kids when it comes to cleaning up after themselves."

> "That there would be mornings when his breath would stink and the thought of kissing him would repulse me."

> "That it's not always easy to cleave to my husband and make him a priority over my family. Sometimes I just want my mom!"

In hindsight, we could make a wish list of things we'd have wanted to know beforehand. Here are a few items my friends would have put on the list.

"I wish I would have better understood the way a man thinks sexually."

"I wish someone would have told me about Metamucil. I couldn't go to the bathroom our entire honeymoon. I was so nervous about doing something gross in front of my new husband."

"I wish someone would have told us not to get a dog for at least a year after getting married. The dog was the source of many fights."

"I wish I would have had someone else's perspective of our relationship."

One sweet lady commented, "No one told me anything. I wish you had written this book 20 years ago!"

I Should Have Listened

Rebecca, another friend of mine, also gave birth a while back. Unlike Abigail, she *had* been warned about something but had paid little heed. I visited her in the hospital the day after her baby was born, and she was disappointed that she still looked five months pregnant (as most new mothers do).

"I told you it would be like this," I said kindly.

"I know," she moaned, "but I thought I would be the exception to the rule!" As do all of us. And we rarely are.

I asked women to tell me something someone *did* warn them about but they didn't believe until they got married.

"That the cute habits would become annoying habits."

"That your time is not your own anymore."

"That men don't change."

"That I would think to myself at some point, 'Why did
I marry him?' "

Why don't we get more warnings from married women when we're
single? For one thing, they know we won't believe them anyway. Most
of us, in our engaged state, were so high in the clouds, we ignored
anyone who said anything about marriage being a lot of blood, sweat,
and tears. When I was engaged, stuff like that went in one ear and
out the other.

"Maybe in *your* marriage," I thought, "but not in *mine.*"

In my inexperienced mind, marriage was all about love, sex, and
a boatload of wedding gifts.

What About Sex?

Speaking of sex…you'll get an earful later on, but sex plays a big
role in your first year of marriage. Many women come into marriage
with a sexual past—either with their husbands or other men. Others
enter marriage as virginal as they come—and good for them! Some
women are shocked (to say the least) the first time they see their
husbands in the buff.

Dr. Kevin Leman warns men about walking out of the hotel bathroom on their wedding night "nude and giving a full salute," which
he says can be "shocking and horrifying to a woman who has never
even seen an erect penis."[1]

"I guess I'd never really seen a man nude," one girl told me shyly.
"Not even in a picture. I don't know what I expected, but it definitely
wasn't *that.* It's all so…different."

If you opened the wrapping paper that is your husband's underwear, and the contents of the package took some getting used to, I'm
with you. Hopefully you'll learn to love and admire your husband's
manliness—and tell him so!

We all come into marriage with sexual expectations. But we don't usually communicate those with our husband before we're married. We should. We need to find out which expectations are doable and which ones are unrealistic. But even a detailed discussion (handled with care) won't prepare us perfectly.

Dr. Leman comments that when he and his wife, Sande, got married, his expectations were sky-high. "I had saved myself for her," he says, "and now she was going to get all of me, several times a day!"

He comments that surprisingly enough, Sande didn't share his expectations. "She thought that we might actually sleep most of the night," he says. "Imagine that!"[2]

Your husband (or you) may have had similar expectations. I know I did.

Other things you might not expect? We can easily visualize the hot, heavy, horny lovemaking-by-moonlight experience. But what about the time you roll over in bed a full two hours before your alarm is set to go off and discover that hubby is rarin' to go?

Sex is the last thing on your mind.

He yanks off his undies, and you catch a whiff. Did something *die* in there? He throws off the covers, revealing a sun-starved body that looks anything but tempting at the moment. And his breath…ugh.

You feel gross yourself and can't imagine hopping aboard the love train under these circumstances. Your teeth feel gritty, your hair is matted, and hubby is already grabbing for your breasts.

Believe it or not, this type of experience can actually end up being quite satisfying. You just have to shove those sexpectations of yours into a suitcase and sit on the lid.

Marriage and sex—and husbands and wives—aren't always pretty. Making love might be different than you imagined. But it can still be pretty darn cool. And it can keep getting better. More on that in a few chapters. And don't you dare turn there right now, young lady. We have some other lessons to learn first.

Give Me Some Space

As an engaged couple with sex on your minds, it's hard to imagine a point in your relationship when you won't want to be on top of each other. Or even together at all. You'll actually want some space.

Joanne Heim notes that when she and her husband were first engaged, they didn't think having separate interests was appropriate. They did everything together. After they were married, they learned that "it was okay for us to explore life without each other."[3]

I can totally relate, except that Gabe was the one who felt that way. At my parents' kitchen table, two weeks before our wedding, all hell broke loose.

Long story short—Gabe wanted us to spend our entire Christmas break from college together. Our wedding was set for January third. I was hoping to spend a couple days at home—alone—before we got married. He couldn't understand how I could claim to love him yet need time to myself.

"Even when we're married," I argued, "we won't want to spend every waking moment together."

"Why not?" He begged to differ.

I was flabbergasted. The fight was long and hard—the only time I actually considered calling off the wedding. We survived that horrid night, and sure enough, once we were married, Gabe realized how ridiculous it would be to spend every second with each other, even if we could.

Here I sit typing, and he's off in another room playing with his Xbox. Whenever I casually remind him of that memorable squabble, he grins sheepishly and changes the subject.

Married in College

Many marriages face a special challenge in the first year: At least one of the spouses is still in college.

Many parents of college-age kids strongly encourage them to finish school before they get married. But the parents often relent because they would rather have their kids safely married than giving in to inevitable sexual temptation.

Christian young people tend to tie the knot at an earlier age for that very reason. If you're already sleeping with your boyfriend, what's the point of getting hitched? If you can have sex without the commitment, what's the big rush?

On the other hand, if your morals and values tell you "no sex without a marriage license," then waiting until graduation can seem like pure torture to two freshmen in love.

When we got married, I had graduated, but Gabe had three semesters left. With classes during the day, he had no choice but to work all evening, so our time together was limited. For the first nine months, before I got a full-time teaching job, our combined income was sparse and sporadic.

My new job provided adequate and dependable income, but I often resented the fact that I was waking up at 6:00 AM for work—and grading papers late into the evening—while Gabe slept in until his 11:00 class.

Getting married during school worked for us. Gabe had been a typical college guy before—messing around more than he studied. If he wasn't e-mailing or calling me, he and his buddies were playing pranks on security guards and breaking curfew.

After we got married, it didn't seem appropriate to stay out until 5:00 AM with his pals while his wife was at home in his bed (he did try it one last time). So what to do with all his free time while I was working? He actually studied for tests and did his homework! His GPA soared!

Even though school and marriage can work, it's no walk in the park. If you're married and in college right now, take heart. It doesn't last forever. And it will produce some of your marriage's most memorable moments.

If you're in the process of deciding whether to get married now or wait until you're finished with school, carefully calculate the pros and cons of each. Most importantly, pray—separately and together—and follow God's leading.

The whole sexual temptation thing might be a real and valid reason for moving your wedding date up rather than pushing it back. Paul isn't necessarily talking to college students in 1 Corinthians 7:9, but he *could* be: "But if they cannot control themselves, they should marry, for it is better to marry than to burn with passion." Good verse to point out to Mom and Dad in your quest to get married before you graduate.

I showed it to my sister's sophomore-in-college boyfriend last night just to watch his face turn pink. "Hey Daniel, I found a theme verse for you and Steph."

His cheeks stayed rosy the rest of the evening, poor guy. But hey, it was winter, and the boy needed some color.

Are You on the Same Page?

Ideally, before you're married, you will have communicated about life's bigger issues and where each of you stand. You'll calmly discuss them and arrive at compromises you can both live with happily.

Gabe and I did a lousy job of working through several important issues before we got married. We had the same core spiritual and moral values, so we didn't worry about much else. We should have.

For example, I came from a family of four children and always assumed I would have at least four—maybe five or six—kids. Gabe had one brother and liked that just fine. The issue never surfaced until our first baby was born.

After Olivia, we discussed how many more we'd add to our clan, and Gabe commented offhandedly that four was "a herd." After Ava, he thought it was high time we called it quits. It took three years of tearful discussions and silent prayer to come to a consensus.

How many children do you and your husband want? When will you start, and how will you space them? Will you work or stay home with your kids?

Maybe you plan to be childless by choice. If this is the case, I urge you to prayerfully consider your decision not to have children (naturally or by adoption). Of course, this is a very personal decision, and couples may have very good reasons for not raising kids. But in today's society, materialism and self-centeredness are acceptable reasons to remain childless. I disagree wholeheartedly.

And since no birth control is 100 percent effective 100 percent of the time, you must always be prepared for the chance that you might get pregnant. For Christians, abortion is no more an option than murdering our husbands.

There are exceptions, but if God gives you the ability to have children, I believe you should have them. Maybe not a truckload, but at least one or two.

What about pets? Do you envision a couple tiny dogs that will sleep in your bed? A great big dog that needs a backyard of his very own? Fish? Birds? Are you a cat lover? Or do you, like me, despise the entire feline species? (Heartless, I know.)

What about chores, vacations, holidays, meals, and money? How do each of you expect to handle these things? You will find a lot of helpful hints throughout this book concerning the merge of your family backgrounds and expectations, but you really need to discuss these issues with your almost-hubby before you head off to your honeymoon.

My friend Jodie recommends finding a workbook (like *Preparing for Marriage*) to help you work through these topics together during your engagement.[4] She says it worked wonders for her and her husband.

Gabe and I should have picked up one of those handy little workbooks.

The Apartment of Babel

In Genesis 11, everyone on earth is speaking the same language. One day, they all start talking and decide to take advantage of their numbers and common goals. They plan to build themselves a grand city with a fabulous tower that reaches to the heavens. They want to make a name for themselves, to control their own destiny so to speak.

God is not impressed with their self-proclaimed self-sufficiency. He comes down from heaven, confuses their language, and scatters them over the face of the earth. Their city—Babel—is left unfinished, and we've been misunderstanding each other ever since.

Toben and Joanne Heim admit that when they first got married, their apartment might have been called Babel as well. They didn't understand each other's language. A typical scenario. Rarely does a marriage start off with the couple sharing a common tongue.

Going into marriage, my friend Tari admits thinking, "My husband will see things my way, and if not, I can easily convince him my idea is best." Not likely.

You have different thoughts and opinions. You don't understand each other's point of view. You don't pay close enough attention to each other. You hear a message and misinterpret it. Tears and harsh words abound. Feelings get hurt on a daily basis.

You each bring your own experience and prior knowledge to the marriage, not to mention your personality, attitude, and outlook on life.

Miss Communication will be a frequent guest in your home, at least for the first year or two (or six). You won't mean to invite her over so often, of course. In fact, you probably won't *invite* her at all. She'll show up unannounced and quite unwelcome.

Unfortunately, even though you'll want to ignore her, you won't be able to. You'll have to deal with her until she gets the hint and leaves. But she'll be back.

Just last night, I asked Gabe an honest and (I thought) unpretentious question. Enter Miss Communication (without even knocking). Gabe immediately became defensive, thinking I was being critical. I tried over and over again to explain myself clearly, to the point of exasperation. I ended up crying and praying silently in another room.

Then I thought of a way to more effectively express my intended meaning. It worked. We talked through it some more, and we resolved the issue and dropped it.

As it turned out, and often does, we actually shared the same opinion and didn't realize it. Miss Communication—the little twerp. Both of us felt attacked until we got on the same page.

One key to good communication is truly listening to your husband. It's not easy to do, but it can save you a world of trouble. Someone once said that God gave us one tongue and two ears so we could listen twice as much as we speak. Not a bad theory.

For me, talking is much easier than listening. I often get bored listening to others, but I could listen to myself for hours. Funny how that works. If I want to be a good communicator and wife, I need to listen to what my husband has to say.

When Gabe talks to me, I'm often intent on interrupting him, pointing out his errors, squeezing in my two cents. Never mind his feelings and ideas. When I don't listen, I'm communicating that he's not important to me. I can *say* he is, but it doesn't mean squat if I don't show it. Sometimes our ears speak louder than our mouths.

You'll be missing out on a lot of neat ideas and perspectives if the only person you listen to is *you*. None of us has all the answers. Once you start really listening to people—namely your hubby—you'll be surprised at what a great experience it can be.

You'll eventually get the hang of this whole communication thing. You'll learn each other's language—even create a dialect the two of you can share. It takes time though, so hang in there. Language school can be a killer.

What If I'm Miserable?

My friend Katie will commemorate one year of marriage next week, but her anniversary won't be cause for celebration.

"I hate being married," she told me recently. "My marriage is awful." Her tone of voice suggested indifference, but the twinge of pain in her eyes belied her toughness.

When Katie became pregnant, she and Kyle immediately got engaged. Three months later, they were married. And miserable.

"We didn't even want to get married," Katie told me. By the time Katie's baby boy was born, her marriage was in the pits. They were drowning in debt with a newborn to care for, and they couldn't even get along.

"Kyle goes to parties," Katie told me. "He drinks. I don't trust him with the baby. I never leave the two of them alone. We can't pay our bills. He's sitting around waiting for a 'good job.' Even McDonald's would be better than nothing! But he won't do it."

I have only heard Katie's side of the story, so I want to be careful not to pass judgment on her husband. I know both parties are at fault.

"Sometimes I just want to sign that piece of paper and get out," she sighed. "My baby and I will be fine."

I was at a loss for words. I didn't want to glibly offer the first words that came to mind: "God can work things out. Just hang in there, keep praying, and be the best wife you can be." Easy for me to say—I'd never been in her shoes.

I felt like saying, "Go ahead and get out, Katie. Your marriage was a mistake. Move back home with your parents and get your life back. You deserve a fresh start. No one should have to endure what you're going through—it's just too much to ask. This is your only chance at happiness."

I didn't say that. I nodded. I listened. I sympathized. And the next day, I wrote her a letter, gently explaining what I felt God had to say about honoring our marriage commitment.

I shared with her an example of a woman I know who was in Katie's exact situation nearly 30 years ago. Today, after many difficult years, her marriage is flourishing. Her husband is in love with both his wife and the Lord. God has richly rewarded her decision to honor her marriage vows, even when it was beyond difficult.

I pray for Katie often—and for her marriage. I know her life won't be easy if she sticks it out with Kyle—but God deals in miracles even now. I know He can heal this bruised and broken relationship. He's in the business of doing that sort of thing every day.

If you, like me, have difficulty relating to Katie, find someone like her and commit to pray for her.

On the other hand, if your story mirrors hers more closely than you'd like to admit, take heart. Find a godly Christian woman who will pray for you and help you work toward restoration. Get some counseling. God can heal your marriage—even if the fracture seems irreparable.

A Tough First Year

My friend Rachel has a good marriage but had a tough first year. She struggled with a new teaching job that was difficult. Her husband, Dave, was a youth pastor, and only after a full year did Rachel feel a part of his ministry. She left her family in another state and had no close friends nearby. She learned to lean on God—and on her husband.

"What stands out in my mind," Rachel says, "is that Dave was faithful to me. He cried and prayed with me. It humbled me because he was being the strong one. He took purposeful steps to make me a part of his ministry, and people slowly started seeing us as a team. When I became dangerously ill with an inner ear infection and threw up repeatedly, Dave sat on the floor in the bathroom and held me."

Rachel learned a lot about herself that year. She realized how much trust she always had in her family and the importance of transferring that trust to her husband. God helped her do just that.

I'm sure Rachel wouldn't want to go back and relive her first year of marriage with all its challenges, but neither do I think she would trade it for the world.

"It was a hard year with the spiritual warfare and everything being new for me, but it was good for our marriage," she says. "Even in my spiritual and physical struggles, Dave loved me. God protected me. Praise Him!"

If your first year of marriage has been tough, try to look at those trials in light of how they've helped you grow. Not easy to do. Very few of us welcome hardships with open arms—all in the name of character development. But if you are able to grow stronger in your faith and closer to Christ, then those tough times are ultimately a blessing.

Smoothin' Those Rough Edges

In their book *Happily Ever After,* Toben and Joanne Heim use a great analogy. When we get married, they say, we're like square paving stones. The goal of marriage is to make us round and smooth.

The first year knocks off all our corners, leaving rough edges. With each passing year, we smooth those edges out until we have the result we'd been hoping for.[5]

What kinds of things break our corners off? Fights, unmet expectations, family differences, miscommunication, sex—just about everything we're going to talk about in this book.

If you're still in your first year of marriage and your stone is nothing but jagged, scratchy, painful edges—take heart! It takes time to make our marriages round and polished. Even after many years, pieces still chip off and need to be leveled out again. There's no time like the present to break out that giant nail file and start smoothing some marital edges!

Part Two

Loving Unselfishly

3

It's Not About Me

Do nothing out of selfish ambition or vain conceit,
but in humility consider others better than yourselves.
Each of you should look not only to your own interests,
but also to the interests of others.

PHILIPPIANS 2:3-4

Believe it or not, *you* are not the main point of your marriage. And *I* am not the point of mine. Shocking, I know. A rude awakening—and why wouldn't it be? After all, you *were* the point of your engagement, your wedding planning, and The Big Day.

You were the one with the sparkling new diamond that people incessantly admired. *You* were the belle of the bridal showers your family and friends gave you. Even the wedding was all about *you*— the ravishing bride in a gorgeous gown of flowing white with yards of lace, beading, and tulle. Who notices the groom in his off-the-rack, rented tux? It was *your* day, done *your* way. You, you, you.

Then you got married, and your husband neglected to treat you as the princess you are—the princess you'd been for as long as you could remember. After being the center of the universe, coming back down to earth can cause quite a crash.

Selfless Choices

"You have *no* idea what a hard day I've had!" you lament to your husband as you walk in the door from work. With a moan, you raise the back of your hand to your forehead and collapse onto the couch like you've been mortally wounded. Your day was rough, and you want pity, sympathy, and an offer to rub your aching feet.

How about this less-common scenario? Your day was rough, but you take a deep breath and walk through the door. You smile, put your tough day behind you, and ask your husband about his. And you actually listen when he tells you about it. And refrain from interjecting after every half-sentence, "You think *that's* bad! Well, let me tell you…"

Many times a day we're faced with the choice to be selfish or selfless. Which will it be?

Last week, we took a 45-minute car trip, and Gabe was driving—the perfect opportunity for me to work on this book. Less than 20 seconds into the drive, Gabe says, "So, do you understand the rules for Texas Hold 'Em?"

I replace my pen cap with a sigh. Choice time. *Write* about marriage (what I *feel* like doing) or *work* on my marriage (what I *should* be doing).

"Uh…if I say no, I don't understand the rules, are you going to explain them in laborious detail to me?" I ask, praying he'll get the hint that this would be an absolute waste of my precious time.

"It'll just take two minutes."

I put down my pen and give him my full attention. Good choice. It did only take a few minutes (eight—I counted).

I wish these unselfish choices came more naturally, but they don't. I always feel that pull to do what *I* want to do. Marriage is one big decision to throw selfishness and independence out the window. I'm a woman who knows what I want—and I have a pretty good idea how to go about getting it. Putting my husband first just messes up my plans—and goes completely against my nature.

Once we're married, we tend to start looking at our husbands with one thing in mind—what can you do for me? When we think they aren't doing enough, we start criticizing and finding fault. Regardless of how hard hubby tries, he falls short.

"So we make it our goal to please him," Paul writes in 2 Corinthians 5:9. Before I do anything in life, I should ask myself whether or not it would please God. Not easy. It's easier to serve myself than Gabe. It's easier to ignore his needs when I'm tired. It's easier to get the last verbal jab in than to be quiet.

Paul's not finished. "Those who live should no longer live for themselves but for him who died for them and was raised again" (2 Corinthians 5:15). It's easier to live for me than God.

Holy, Not Happy

The inside flap of the book jacket had me hooked. "Scores of books have been written that offer guidance for building the marriage of your dreams. But what if God's primary intent for your marriage isn't to make you happy...but holy?"[1]

The holy-not-happy concept is the premise of Gary Thomas' *Sacred Marriage.* If happiness is your primary goal for marriage, being with one man the rest of your life isn't going to cut it. Are we happy with one pair of jeans our whole life? One couch? One car? We can't very well trade in our marriage every two years!

If we view happiness as our ultimate goal, then every challenge we face will be a huge roadblock keeping us from our destination. The idea is to ask God, "How can I use the challenges of marriage to help me grow closer to You?"

If I had my way, He'd just take the struggles away. Yet I have to admit that I do my best growing through the tough times, not the easy, breezy ones.

I asked my survey-taking friends to tell me what areas of marriage they find difficult—what challenges they face day in and day out.

"Not to be cross when under pressure."

"Not being selfish—wanting the best for my husband instead of myself."

"Focusing on his positive attributes."

"Doing things that are special for each other continually."

"Ignoring his annoying habits!"

"Give and take—making sure we do things each other enjoys."

"Keeping communication open."

"Not getting into a rut of taking each other for granted."

"Our spiritual connection."

"Nagging."

"Making time for a physical relationship."

"Being genuinely interested in my husband's goals and dreams."

"The level of respect we show each other."

We're all about getting something for nothing. Reaping the benefits without the hard work. Ten simple steps to this, five easy steps to that. I can't guarantee you a problem-free marriage or tell you how to have a better marriage with less effort. Marriage isn't simple. And it's not easy. Sure, you can do some practical things to improve your marriage. But the bottom line is this—become more like Christ, and you'll find your marriage more fulfilling. Your marriage may not change, but *you* will. That will make all the difference.

Let me warn you—this is not easy! One day, you'll do an

amazing job and be the best darn wife in the country. The very next day, your sinful nature is going to kick back in, and you'll be stinkin' up the place with your haughtiness and rudeness. Take it from me, a girl who often stinks.

God never intended for us to "arrive" in our marriages. That's not even the goal. The goal is to take each trial and challenge and use it to help us grow more like Christ. God didn't create marriage to make us happy. He created it to bring us to Him.

God's Standards

I have good news and bad news. The bad news is that when we mess up, God doesn't lower the standards for us. The good news is that He offers us something else—grace. Really, the bad news isn't bad news at all. We wouldn't want a God who was forever lowering the bar.

The world does this all the time. Staying in a marriage takes too much work, so we make divorce a culturally acceptable solution. Want sex but no commitment? No problem. Too hard to climb the corporate ladder with complete honesty and integrity? Just step on a few toes and break a few rules as long as no one gets hurt…too badly.

A lot of material out there says, "So you're not a good wife? That's okay. As long as you try. It's too much to ask for a wife to submit all the time or always put her husband first or to put 100 percent effort into her marriage every single day. Just do what you can."

One hundred percent effort is *not* too much to ask. It's exactly what God requires of us. He commands us to be holy, set apart, without sin. When we do mess up, which is about once every five minutes on some days, He offers us His grace. But that's not the same as lowering His holy standards. He can't do that.

Think of it as a race. We're aiming for the finish line. When we trip and fall, God does not move the tape closer to us, regardless of how much we beg. It stays put. He doesn't let us quit the race and take home a "participant" ribbon.

What He does do is help us up, dust us off, and give us a gentle push on our way. He has given us an assignment—to be holy. He won't change the assignment when we fail. He'll just keep helping us up and giving us second, third, and fifty-sixth chances to get it right.

Becoming More like Christ

My cousin Kyla idolized me when we were kids. No matter what I did, wore, said, or ate, she wanted to do, wear, say, and eat it too. If I wanted to skip around the yard, so did Kyla. If I wore purple leg warmers, so did Kyla. She didn't make a move without checking with me. She was my shadow, my echo, my mirror image.

Kyla's missionary family of seven lived with our family of six for more than a year. Things ran fairly smoothly even though nine of us were under the age of twelve.

One day, my aunt became fed up with Kyla's copycat antics. Kyla actually began eating food she hated just because I liked it. And she scorned some of her favorite foods because I didn't like them.

"Enough already," Kyla's mom told her. "Stop trying to be just like Marla. This is ridiculous."

Her words made no impact on Kyla. So Auntie came up with a plan. She whispered her scheme into my ear that evening. I had to smile.

"Kids," my aunt announced, as we gathered around the supper table. "Who wants a candy bar with their meal?" Eight hands shot in the air, amidst squeals of delight.

I kept my arm at my side and my eyes on Kyla. As soon as she realized she had done something on her own, she quickly turned to me for approval. When she saw that my hand wasn't flailing in the air like the others, she shot hers down.

"What? No candy bar, Kyla?" her mother asked.

"No thank you, ma'am," Kyla said sheepishly, trying to hide her disappointment.

My aunt couldn't believe it. No child turns down a candy bar for supper. This was turning into a disease.

"Okay then, how about this?" said her exasperated mother. "Marla's having a pile of poop for dinner! Let me dish one up for you too!"

The Moral of the Story

If we imitated Christ as closely as Kyla imitated me, can you imagine the impact we would have on our marriages? My heart is saddened when I think how rarely my thoughts and actions truly mirror Christ's.

"You are either becoming more like Christ every day or you're becoming less like Him," Stormie Omartian says.[2]

Our highest calling as Christians is to follow Christ—to imitate Him, become more like Him in every way. First Peter 2:21 says, "To this you were called, because Christ suffered for you, leaving you an example, that you should follow in his steps."

Jesus said to His disciples in Luke 9:23, "If anyone would come after me, he must deny himself and take up his cross daily and follow me."

Kyla denied herself to follow me. She pushed her own desires aside in order to want what I wanted, to love what I loved. She went against her own nature in her quest to emulate me.

How do we go about imitating Christ? Think of people who impersonate celebrities for a living. They learn as much as they can about a person. They watch him in action, listen to him talk, study his mannerisms, take notes, spend time with him, and practice acting the way he does.

If you want to imitate Christ, learn more about Him. Spend time with Him. Read His Word. Study His life in the Bible. Spend time talking to others about Him. Take notes on what you learn so you don't forget it. And practice, practice, practice acting as He would. Deny your disordered desires and look to Christ to see what His will is for your life.

Ephesians 5:1-2 (MSG) says, "Watch what God does, and then you do it, like children who learn proper behavior from their parents. Mostly what God does is love you. Keep company with him and learn a life of love. Observe how Christ loved us. His love was not cautious but extravagant. He didn't love us in order to get something from us but to give everything of himself to us. Love like that." Tall order, but God promises that we've been given everything we need to live a godly life.

Our goal as Christians is for others to look at us and immediately see Jesus.

Through God's Eyes

Becoming more like Christ includes looking at your husband through God's eyes. Pretend that you've decided to eavesdrop for a moment on a conversation between me and God—one that transpires entirely too often.

"Honestly, God, you know Gabe needs to change more than I do."

"I know no such thing."

"Oh, come on, Lord, let's not kid ourselves. He's the one who loses his temper more, reads his Bible less, watches more R-rated movies, prays less often…"

"Are you finished?"

"Um…sure."

"First of all, I told you not to judge. I'll take care of that. And secondly, do you think that when I look at My children, I see all their faults and give each fault a rating? Then add up the totals and compare each child with another?"

"Hey, that's a really good idea! I wonder where I'd rank!"

"Lower than you think, I'm afraid, if that's how you want to do things. My dear child, where do I begin? How about the fifty-fifth chapter of Isaiah, starting with verse eight? Why don't you look that up?"

"Um…okay. Here it is. It says, "'For my thoughts are not your thoughts, neither are your ways my ways,' declares the LORD."

"Keep going."

"As the heavens are higher than the earth, so are my ways higher than your ways and my thoughts than your thoughts."

"What do you think of that?"

"Well, yeah, of course Your thoughts are higher than mine, but—"

"That means I don't always go about things the way you might."

"Yeah, I guess—"

"And it doesn't say My thoughts and ways are merely *different* from yours. What does it say they are?"

"Higher."

"Yes, higher. Better. The best, in fact. The only way. Are you willing to accept that and trust Me?"

"Um…yeah, I trust You. But how can I look at Gabe with all his faults and not try to change them?"

"My dear child, you're forgetting something very important. Because of My Son's sacrifice on the cross, all who accept Him as their Savior have their sins washed away by His blood. When I look at you, I see My Son. When I look at Gabe, I see My Son—not glaring faults and terrible sins. I see the precious blood of My Son, shed for you and Gabe. Looking at Gabe through My eyes will make all the difference."

Praying for Your Husband

If you haven't read Stormie O'Martian's *The Power of a Praying Wife,* I encourage you to do so. She suggests that the first prayer you should pray for your husband—before you pray for his spiritual growth, work, or finances—is for his wife. If we want God to answer our prayers, we have to come to Him purely. That means examining our own hearts and confessing any sins we're hanging on to—big or small.

Stormie says her heart had to be "softened, humbled, pummeled, molded, and reconstructed" before God even started working on her husband. She "had to learn to see things according to the way God saw them"—not how she thought they should be.[3]

This marriage thing isn't about Gabe becoming a better spouse to me (darn it). It's about God perfecting me through trials and often (quite often!) choosing to use my husband as an instrument in my refining process.

That's why I've found it's so vital to *pray* about changes in my husband's life rather than nag. Prayer makes my heart more ready to hear what God has to say to *me* through all of it. When I nag, oddly enough, I never seem to bring about change. If, by some chance, Gabe does decide to change his ways, I get all the "credit" for it.

When I pray to God with my mouth shut and Gabe makes a change for the better, *he* thinks he did it himself, and *I* know it was God. Everybody wins. Often, as an added bonus, Gabe will give *God* the credit, knowing that the change came from outside his own abilities and efforts.

Why does praying work and nagging not? Maybe God doesn't want any confusion over who gets the glory when He touches hearts and changes lives. When nagging produces any sort of result, we get prideful. And our husbands, more often than not, feel resentful.

Praying for someone who has hurt you is tough, especially if that person is your husband. Praying for Gabe is the last thing I want to do when I'm feeling hurt or angry. Smacking him, kicking him, throwing something at him, cussing at him, destroying his Xbox, never speaking to him again as long as I live—all much higher on the list.

You'll be amazed, though, at how God can use the act of praying for your husband to soften your heart toward him. When we can't love our husbands on our own, God can do it through us, using our prayers.

Ask God to help you let go of anger and bitterness you have toward your husband, even if it seems justified. If you're holding yourself back from him emotionally or physically because you just can't seem to forgive him, it's time to release those feelings to God. Or ask Him to rip them away from you if you can't let go.

Christ loves our husbands with a love we could never reproduce on our own, but we can ask Him to help us love our husbands the way He does.

Stormie admits she tried everything *but* praying until she realized that all that other stuff—arguing, pleading, ignoring, the silent treatment—was futile.

"It's laying down all claim to power in and of yourself," she says, "and relying on God's power to transform you, your husband, your circumstances, and your marriage."[4]

Give your husband to God—He's much better at getting people to do His bidding.

Plank in Your Eye

Aesop once wrote, "The injuries we do and those we suffer are seldom weighed on the same scales." I often have two sets of standards—one for me and one for Gabe.

As a teacher, I sometimes laughed when two students came to me to resolve a fight. The discrepancies in their accounts of what happened were humorous. Each one tried his darnedest to make the other person out to be the bad guy and himself completely innocent. I've found myself employing the same tactics with Gabe.

When we do something wrong, we downplay our mistake as best we can. When we are the ones who are wronged, we exaggerate the offense. This bad habit (read: sin) gets worse as you make the transition from fiancée to wife. Engaged and enraptured with love, you graciously overlook his tiny, insignificant faults. When you get married, those faults bloom and spread overnight.

Jesus preached a sermon in Matthew 7 about judging others' flaws without seeing the glaring faults in your own life. "How can you say to your brother, 'Let me take the speck out of your eye,' when all the time there is a plank in your own eye?" (verse 4).

If you're thinking, "My husband is the one with the plank," bingo! You're exactly who Jesus is talking to!

One woman told me her view of sin used to be all mixed up. She was critical and judgmental but didn't think anything of it. But her husband's swearing and temper and TV viewing habits—now those were some bad sins.

We wives need to realize that "little" sins like unforgiveness, jealousy, bitterness, withholding love, inattentiveness, self-pity, anger, and holding grudges aren't so little after all. In fact, God considers sins of the heart to be just as bad as "action" sins like swearing, lying, and cheating. They may even be worse.

Drop the Fruit and No One Gets Hurt

Ever heard of the fruit of the Spirit—love, joy, peace, patience, kindness, goodness, faithfulness, gentleness, and self-control? I used to think that fruit was the result of my own human efforts—which repeatedly failed. Then I read the "fruit passage" in The Message.

> But what happens when we live God's way? He brings gifts into our lives, much the same way that fruit appears in an orchard—things like affection for others, exuberance about life, serenity. We develop a willingness to stick with things, a sense of compassion in the heart, and a conviction that a basic holiness permeates things and people. We find ourselves involved in loyal commitments, not needing to force our way in life, able to marshal and direct our energies wisely (Galatians 5:22–23).

Voila! I saw the fruit in a whole new light. What made the difference? The word *gifts.* These qualities aren't things we have to strive and strain to achieve. God *gives* us the ability to carry them out when we let His Spirit have His way in our lives. We surrender—give up trying—and that's when the fruit "magically" appears.

We're worthless without God and can do nothing apart from Him. We can't be good wives or good anythings for that matter. What we can do *with* God is a completely different story. So we throw up our hands, admit that we're hopeless without Him, and ask Him to fill us with His Holy Spirit.

I believe that when we accept Christ as our Savior and Lord, the Holy Spirit comes to live inside us permanently. He's a guest in our home, and we decide what part He plays in our lives.

Will we push Him into a back room or the basement and tell Him He can stay but not to get in our way? Or will we welcome Him into every room of our home, asking Him to feel free to make use of everything we own, explore our closets, drawers, nooks, and crannies, to live as part of our family as we converse and share with Him deeply on a daily basis? How much of you are you going to let Him have?

And when it comes to those nine juicy pieces of fruit, they're yours for the picking! Just as a tree doesn't have to *do* anything to produce fruit, neither do you!

So often I find myself trying to tackle my problems, my day, my marriage conflicts by myself. As long as I see a way to do it myself, I'm not gonna go with Plan B—God's way. Only when I reach the end of my rope do I cry out to God, "Help me!"

The same problems creep up and overwhelm me. I make the same mistakes again and again. I resolve to change, to do better next time, to make a lasting transformation, but alas! I cannot do it!

With the Holy Spirit's help, on the other hand, I am invincible.

I'm Not My Husband's Holy Spirit

Convicting others of sin isn't on our job description, yet how often do we try to take the Holy Spirit's rightful place in our husband's life? As if our Christian duty is to remind our husband that he has sinned, correct him when he messes up, and show him the right way to go.

For years, Kathy nagged her husband, Bob, to be more of a spiritual leader in their home. Then she felt God telling her to stop trying to be God in her husband's life. That wasn't her place, and besides, it wasn't working! She sensed God telling her to back off, that she didn't need to keep Bob going.

She also realized that spiritual leadership isn't always measured by our standards. If she could turn back the clock, she says, "I'd stop trying to make my husband into the spiritual giant I wanted. I'd be more aware of the manifestation of a deepening walk with the Lord through his actions and the way he treated me and others, instead of how much he read his Bible. I was too legalistic."[5]

We wives can intimidate our husbands by our spiritual verbosity. We don't often realize that our marriages and our spiritual lives don't belong in separate compartments. Kathy began connecting with

Bob through everyday events. They soon began praying about those mundane things for each other, which led to praying for their family as a couple. Soon, their spiritual lives began to weave together.

Kathy realized that just because she didn't see Bob deepening his spiritual walk didn't mean he wasn't doing it. That hit home with me. I thought for the first few years of marriage that if I didn't do my darnedest to get Gabe on track spiritually, I wasn't being a good wife *or* a good Christian. Too bad nothing in the Bible supports my faulty thinking.

I got frustrated when Gabe didn't spend as much time in God's Word as I did. I assumed I was more spiritual than he was, but that wasn't necessarily the case. Yes, Gabe needed to read his Bible more, but I needed to be living it out. Neither of us was doing it completely right.

Romans 2:13 (msg) tells us that "merely hearing God's law is a waste of your time if you don't do what he commands. Doing, not hearing, is what makes the difference with God."

"I used to be so self-centered," one woman said. "Now I love my husband for exactly who God made him to be. I don't have my own agenda anymore for life. I enjoy every day for all it has to offer, as Christ wants it."

"I'm not always trying to change my husband now," another woman told me. "I let God do that. I've stopped pushing buttons that cause problems. I don't care so much about petty little details that don't matter."

In the last seven years, God has done an amazing work in Gabe's heart—with no help from me.

Husband-Seeking Love

Marriage is give and take. Sometimes it's even give and give. But it should never be take and take and take some more. Remember the verse from the beginning of the chapter? We should be looking to the interests of others and not only our own.

Has your husband asked you to do something with him that you've put off because the activity doesn't appeal to you?

First Corinthians 13:5 tells us that love is not self-seeking. Self-seeking means that my primary concern is what makes *me* happy. Let's eat at *my* favorite restaurant, watch *my* favorite movie, play *my* favorite game. I want to spend all *my* time on *my* own selfish pursuits rather than on things that make Gabe happy.

Many husbands wish their wives weren't so busy and would just sit down and watch TV or a movie with them. Gabe is one of those husbands!

The trouble is that I have a hard time sitting still. It's tough for me to watch an entire two-hour movie without getting up to fold laundry, put away dishes, or check e-mail. Maybe you can relate. Let's just sit down and watch a movie!

We women bond with each other by sharing our feelings. Men typically *do* things together. We *talk*. They *do*. We want our husbands to open up to us, to share their innermost feelings with us. Our husbands want to bond with us too, but they don't always want to talk. They want us to *do* things with them—and not just sex either!

Gabe would like me to do some things with him that I just don't enjoy, like play video games or a game of chess. But whether I do something only he likes or something we both like, it's important that we do something together!

Some husbands enjoy their golf or softball games with just the boys, but some would love for their wives to get involved in some type of sport with them. Have you tried tennis? Running? Hunting? Roller hockey? Racquetball? Golf? Fishing? Croquet?

Why don't we like to try new things? Laziness? Fear? Don't want to rock the boat? Well, it's time to get over it! What's the worst that can happen? You won't like your new activity. At least you tried! And you won't know until you do.

"Don't knock it till you've tried it" can be your new motto for your marriage. What a great husband-seeking way to show love!

The Love Chapter Test

So we know that love isn't self-seeking, but 1 Corinthians 13 lists a bunch of other things love isn't—and is—as well. As I read through Paul's letter to the people in Corinth this week, the words of that familiar thirteenth chapter hit me in a brand-new way. I'd always found the "love is this, love is that" verses to be beautiful sentiments—I even had them printed on our wedding announcements. But this time, the Holy Spirit prompted me to read these words with a fresh perspective.

I digested each phrase slowly and carefully, letting the words sink in. Love is patient. Love is kind. It does not envy. Hmm...Evidently, love wasn't just a fuzzy feeling but was characterized by at least 15 specific, identifiable, measurable *actions*.

Then I had a disturbing revelation. If I'm not *doing* all these things, what does that mean? Are the words "I love you" nothing more than a resounding gong—empty and meaningless—if I don't back them up? If I fail the "love chapter test," do I not love my husband? Let's take a look.

Love is patient. Too bad we couldn't start off with an easier one. Patience means not expecting perfection from my husband immediately but allowing him time to learn and grow.

I might think that, since God is all-powerful, surely He could work some teensy little changes in my husband. And I'd be right—He can. But He may have some greater purpose in mind, which undoubtedly includes molding my character to conform to His own.

Romans 5:3-5 (MSG) says, "We continue to shout our praise even when we're hemmed in with troubles, because we know how troubles can develop passionate patience in us, and how that patience in turn forges the tempered steel of virtue, keeping us alert for whatever God will do next."

Patience means waiting for God's perfect timing—without complaining—even when His schedule doesn't even slightly resemble the one in my day planner.

Love is kind. Kindness is a little easier than patience. Unless I'm tired. Or in a bad mood. Or ready to start my period. Or just sick of being nice all the time.

Kindness means allowing only positive, uplifting words to come out of my mouth when speaking to my husband or about my husband to others. Love chooses to be kind when I would much rather say something like "You are such a jerk!" or "Just shut up and leave me alone!" or "Don't tell me what to do!"

Kindness can mean complimenting my husband on his physical features, his spiritual growth, the blessings he brings to our marriage, his talents and abilities, or his considerate treatment of me or others.

Kindness shows up in my actions as well. Being kind can be giving my husband a back scratch when I'm tired, picking up after him when he's in a hurry, or taking out the trash (without complaining) when he forgets.

Kindness might be bringing him a Coke while he's watching a football game, making his favorite meal, or writing him a note of encouragement and tucking it into his pants pocket on his way out the door.

It does not envy. Love does not envy when people praise my husband's accomplishments and overlook mine. Love does not envy when my husband's job takes him outside and he gets a nice tan while I'm stuck inside an office all day. Love does not envy when my husband's metabolism works three times faster than mine.

How about a different twist? Love doesn't envy another woman because her husband has character traits mine lacks. Love doesn't envy the fabulous home that someone else's husband paid for on his six-figure salary.

Envy says, "Lord, I don't like how you're providing for me. I'd rather have what *she* has." Envy is forever focusing on others—what they have and you don't. Proverbs 14:30 says, "A heart at peace gives life to the body, but envy rots the bones."

The antidote to envy is focusing on God—being content with, and grateful for, the home, possessions, husband, and life He has blessed me with.

It does not boast. Boasting—what a temptation. When my husband is messing something up and I know exactly how to do it right, why shouldn't I pipe up, step in, take over, and show him my stuff?

Love never brags about my possessions or achievements. When I boast about these things, I'm revealing that my identity is wrapped up in what I have and what I've done.

God wants us to focus on who we are *in Him.* When we're secure in our identity as dearly loved children of our heavenly Father, none of those other things matter. All that matters is that God loves us. We belong to Him.

Ephesians 2:8-9 reminds us that we were saved through grace and that it was all from God, not because of ourselves, "so that no one can boast."

It is not proud. Love is not too proud to admit I'm wrong. To ask my husband for help when I need it. To say, "I don't know the solution to this problem." To admit, "Your idea worked out a lot better than mine would have." Love is willing to hear my husband's perspective.

Love doesn't always have to be right or emerge the victor. Love never says, "I'd rather be right than forgiven." Love doesn't have a big head, nor does it exhibit false humility.

Love doesn't say (or think), "I deserve better than you," or "My time is too valuable to spend it doing this for you," or "I am so much more spiritual than you."

Contrary to popular opinion, love does *not* mean never having to say you're sorry. Real love not only says "I'm sorry" but also swallows its pride and asks humbly for forgiveness.

It is not rude. How many times have I spat out mean comments to Gabe without thinking, or even worse, in a deliberate attempt to hurt his feelings? "Out of the overflow of the heart the mouth speaks" (Matthew 12:34), and I have to constantly ask God to help me get my heart right with Him. He is not pleased when rudeness gushes from my heart and cascades off my tongue.

It is not self-seeking. We pretty much covered this base in the section on husband-seeking love. Like it or not, marriage isn't all about *me.* It's not even *mostly* about me.

It is not easily angered. Closely related to "rude" is its cousin "easily angered." In the next chapter, I'll share some painful examples from personal experience.

It keeps no record of wrongs. Love doesn't say, "He made a rude comment to me yesterday, so I'll be sure to say something mean to him today." Or "You've left your glass on the end table the past four nights, and I'm sick of cleaning up after you."

Love doesn't bring up past offenses every time I get in an argument. Love doesn't keep a running tab of everything my husband has ever done wrong. Love doesn't carry around a scorecard, as if my marriage was a game of miniature golf.

We will never be happy living in the past—holding on to bitterness and anger. When we let those go, we can live in the present and move forward into a productive, joyful life.

Think of the hurts and wrongs done to you in your marriage as being written on a dry-erase board, not chiseled in stone. And erase that board often!

Love does not delight in evil. Love doesn't encourage my husband to break rules, the law, or promises he's made. Love doesn't smile in satisfaction or secretly get excited when my husband makes a mistake or commits a sin.

Love doesn't push my husband's buttons to his limit and then delight in the fact that he said something he shouldn't, so now I have a valid reason to be angry with him.

In order to please God, we should love what He loves and hate what He hates. God loves people, and He loves truth. He hates all that is evil.

But rejoices with the truth. Love means supporting my husband when he tells the truth at work, even if his integrity costs him his job. Love is thankful when my husband confronts me with the truth about my actions and attitudes—even if it hurts. Love means never lying to my husband—no matter what.

Refuse to buy into Satan's lies about your marriage and your husband—"You deserve better than him. You don't *really* have to submit to your husband. If you aren't fulfilled, get out of this marriage and find someone who will really make you happy."

Believe God's truth instead. "I created your husband in My image. I want you to see him as I see him. Honor him. Serve him. Submit to him. Be faithful to him. Love him."

It always protects. I once played a game of tug-of-war with a two-year-old at a bonfire in the woods. It was great fun, until two days later when I discovered the disturbing truth about our tug-of-war rope (a vine I'd found wrapped around a tree). As I peered in the mirror, one eye swollen shut, a vicious rash wrapped around my face, I realized we had been playing with poison—ivy to be exact. Me, the veteran camp counselor, trained in the art of recognizing forest dangers. I had done a lousy job of protecting Sebastian, my two-year-old buddy, from potential harm. Thankfully, God had created the little cherub with an immunity to forest poisons.

God expects us to protect our husbands from poison as well—the poison of slander and negativity. Love protects my husband's reputation, his pride, and his feelings. Love protects him from the criticism of others—and myself!

Don't be like the careless girl who played with mysterious vines. Always be on the alert for things that could potentially hurt your husband.

Always trusts. Love doesn't call my husband every hour while he's out of town to make sure he's not cheating on me. Love lets my husband know that I have enough faith in him to allow him to make decisions for our family. Love lets other people know how much I trust my husband.

Always hopes. Love says, "I believe in you. I know you can do this!" Love sees the best in my husband and has confidence he can become even better. Love is always looking forward to a wonderful future with him, even when things look dim. Love says, "We can get through this. God has bountiful blessings in store."

Always perseveres. Love remains steadfast in the face of unpleasant circumstances. Love doesn't give up when my husband messes up yet again. Love doesn't throw in the towel. Love keeps on going until the end. Love doesn't consider divorce a viable option.

"Consider it pure joy my brothers, whenever you face trials of many kinds," James says, "because you know that the testing of your faith develops perseverance. Perseverance must finish its work so that you may be mature and complete, not lacking anything" (1:2-3).

Trials in marriage serve a vital purpose—to mature and complete us. A marriage characterized by joyful perseverance is an enduring testimony to the world around us.

Love never fails. Love is for always. Forever. Unending. Till death do us part.

Just last week, my grandma and I stood by my grandpa's hospital bed a few hours before he left us to go be with Jesus. I ached as I watched Grandma stroke Grandpa's cheek, kiss his forehead, and tell him how much she loved him. And I knew she meant it with all of her heart.

They were married for 62 years, five months, and four days. If God had not called Grandpa home, the days, months, and years would still be piling up. Grandma and Grandpa knew what Paul was talking about when he said, "Love never fails."

> Love never gives up. Love cares for others more than self. Love doesn't want what it doesn't have. Love doesn't strut, doesn't have a swelled head, doesn't force itself on others, isn't always "me first," doesn't fly off the handle, doesn't keep score of the sins of others, doesn't revel when others grovel, takes pleasure in the flowering of truth, puts up with anything, trusts God always, always looks for the best, never looks back, but keeps going to the end. Love never dies (1 Corinthians 13:4-8 MSG).

Ten "Easy" Tips for a Happy Marriage

I warned you that I wasn't about to give you five simple steps to a thrilling marriage, but here are some things you can do—they're not easy!—to make your marriage a better place to be.

1. Become less absorbed with yourself.
2. Put your husband's needs before your own.
3. Remember that your happiness is not the point of your marriage.
4. Working hard = a better marriage.

5. Become more like Christ, and your marriage will be more fulfilling.

6. Look at your husband through God's eyes.

7. Pray for your husband—especially those times when you don't like him very much.

8. Ask God to change you.

9. Just give up—surrender your efforts to the Holy Spirit.

10. Love your husband with a 1 Corinthians 13 kind of love.

Ask God specifically to give you the strength and desire to live out some of these suggestions in your marriage. Yes, it will take work, but the best things in life aren't free.

4

Fighting Fairly

*Don't have anything to do with
foolish and stupid arguments, because
you know they produce quarrels.*

2 TIMOTHY 2:23

"Sure, we fight all the time now," an engaged friend told me the other day, "but it's mostly about the wedding and stupid stuff. I know we'll be fine once we're married. We'll probably hardly fight at all."

My face turned red as I struggled not to laugh.

"Um…yeah," I stalled. "You'll probably be fine once you're married. It's so crazy how marriage makes your problems just melt away."

I faked a cough, hiding my smirk with my hand.

She smiled smugly, pleased that I agreed with her so heartily.

"Hey," she said, her eyes lighting up, "you're writing a book about marriage, right?"

"Yep."

"And you're interviewing people who are newly married, right?"

"Sure am."

"Well, why don't you give me a call in a couple months, and I can tell you how marriage is going. You could use me as an example. You know, to help other young women."

"That is a simply smashing idea," I told her. "You'd be *perfect* for my book."

Your First Marital Dispute

If only I had kept a journal of all my fights with Gabe from our honeymoon until now. On a bad day, I could pull out that journal and have a good laugh. I would chuckle at the silly, stupid things we used to argue about (and wonder why we're still fighting about some of them).

I asked women to share the topic of their first marital dispute. Seeing these arguments in print makes us painfully aware of how ridiculous they are. Hardly worth the huffing and puffing, the raised voices, the crossed arms and rolled eyes, and the tears of anger and frustration. Read 'em and weep. Or just smile a knowing smile.

"We couldn't agree on how the towels should be folded."

"I spent his 'hard-earned money' on something 'completely frivolous.'"

"On the way to our honeymoon, I changed lanes without signaling, and Josh got upset at my rudeness to the other drivers."

"Clothes left on the floor."

"He made a joking remark about my broad butt in front of our friends." (Ouch!)

"Comments about each other's families."

"We were playing pool and I kept losing. Jason danced around singing, 'I am the champion.' I threw down my stick and ran to our bedroom. I was so mad."

"He paid for our much-too-expensive honeymoon suite on a credit card."

"I cheered against his Miami Dolphins and gloated when they lost."

"The laundry pile got a tiny bit out of hand."

"He didn't come home when I thought he would, and I was worried sick."

"Jim often went out with the guys after work. He came home late, and I didn't care too much for that. I used to get really mad at him."

"We were married just a week, and a good friend of his came to visit. They left for a while, and I felt so alone and hurt."

One friend told me her first few months of marriage were great. But the next few were filled with "fighting, disappointment, and wondering what I had gotten myself into."

Another friend shared that it was great to be together after a long, separated engagement. "It was difficult, though, especially working out roles in the home. We had more 'fights' in our first year than any of the others," she said.

Drip, Drip, Drip

I was a newlywed who actually liked to fight and quarrel, so my decision to read a chapter a day in Proverbs had started to haunt me. This particular book of the Bible just didn't sit well with me. Verse after verse seemed to fly off the pages and convict me.

Take a look at Proverbs 18:2. "A fool finds no pleasure in understanding but delights in airing his own opinions." Who, me? Delight in my own opinions? Just because I always make sure Gabe knows exactly how I feel about every little thing?

Verse 13 of that chapter says, "He who answers before listening—that is his folly and his shame." So every time I butt in and make sure I have the first (and last) word, that's foolish and shameful? When Gabe asks me something and I answer before he's finished talking, that's not good? What if I finish his sentences for him? Not acceptable?

Oooh, here comes 21:9. "Better to live on the corner of the roof than share a house with a quarrelsome wife." As I nit and pick and start pointless arguments with Gabe, is he thinking, "I'd be better off on the roof than in my own living room?"

And it gets worse in verse 19. "Better to live in a desert than with a quarrelsome and ill-tempered wife." Now Gabe's better off setting up camp with the cacti and Gila monsters than living with me. This stings.

And 27:15—"A quarrelsome wife is like a constant dripping on a rainy day." Time to close the book of Proverbs before I shoot myself.

The only consolation I had was realizing I must not be the only ill-tempered, quarreling, shameful wife in the world, or else Solomon wouldn't have written so many Proverbs on the subject. That's what you get for having so many wives, O wise and wealthy king! What man with any sense wants the trouble of more than one mate?

So I wasn't alone, but that didn't excuse my behavior. Now what was I going to do about it? I could either avoid reading any Scripture that spoke to me as a wife, or I could get busy fixing my faults and ensuring that my attitudes and actions lined up with the principles in God's Word.

I'm afraid that, at least in the beginning, I made the wrong choice more often than not.

A Temper and a Tongue

This book isn't big enough to hold all the stories I could tell about losing my temper with Gabe, so I'll just share a couple. One in particular stands out in my mind.

It was well past midnight. I awoke from a sound sleep as Gabe yanked on my T-shirt. He was frantically mumbling something I couldn't understand.

"What do you want?" I snapped. "I'm trying to sleep!"

"The oven's on!" he shouted. "You left the oven on! I went out to the kitchen to get a drink, and it felt really hot out there! You left the oven on!"

"Well, go turn it off," I growled and rolled back across the bed.

"I don't know how!" he cried. "You come turn it off!"

"For crying out loud! How can you not know how to turn an oven off?" I spat out the words as I stumbled out of bed, tripping on the covers as I made my way to the kitchen.

Sure enough, the oven was on, baking *nothing* at 400 degrees.

"There. Are you happy now?" I glared at him as I turned the knob. "That sure was hard, wasn't it? I'm glad you woke me up for *that!*"

We climbed back into bed, but that wasn't the last I heard about the oven.

"What if the apartment would have burned down?" my overdramatic husband wanted to know. "What if we wouldn't have been able to get out? What if you forget to turn the oven off again? Are you *sure* you turned it all the way off? Can you go out and look again, just to make sure?"

"Are you *insane?* What is your *problem?*" I yelled. "The oven is *off.* There is no halfway off. Off is off! Now go to sleep!"

"Can you please just get up and check?" he had the audacity to ask. "Please. I'll feel so much better if I know for sure. I don't think I'm going to be able to sleep as it is."

I couldn't believe this was happening. I had to get up in four hours, and he wanted *me* to get back up out of bed and make *sure* the oven was off?

I jumped out of bed, stormed into the kitchen, and marched back into the bedroom without even so much as a glance at the oven.

"It's off. Off! Off! Off! Now leave me alone!" My face burned with anger.

"What would we do if the apartment burnt down?" he asked for the fifth time.

"We'd *die!*" I yelled.

I woke the next morning feeling remorseful and ashamed that I had let my tongue take the reins once again.

Gabe was afraid I'd set our home on fire by my carelessness, but the book of James says the tongue is a fire, corrupting the whole person.

Just two days later, I lost it again. The day started out fine. Then I began to get grouchy for no good reason. My bad mood wasn't obvious to the casual observer (that would be my husband) until I began to cook supper. That's when I blew it.

I was boiling water for spaghetti and getting ready to brown the hamburger. So far, so good. My empty stomach was no longer growling but screaming, so I decided to open the jar of sauce and sneak a taste.

It was disgusting. Some Tomato Alfredo concoction—a shower gift from a well-meaning relative. Angrily, I threw it in the trash, flipped off the burner, shoved the hamburger, mushrooms, and olives back in the refrigerator, and slammed the door. Yes, I was raging over a jar of spaghetti sauce.

I stormed around the apartment, taking my frustration out on my husband. He was confused and a bit hurt, but he took it like a man. When he left for work, he asked me nicely if I'd be in a better mood when he got home. I grudgingly obliged but found great comfort in the fact that I'd have three whole hours to bask in my grumpiness first.

My plan went up in smoke as I begin to feel convicted about my attitude after three *minutes*. Gabe and I had received a letter that afternoon from a man who had attended our wedding and was "honored" to be at a wedding that "focused its attention on Jesus Christ." He went on to say, "The two of you have made a great decision in allowing the Lord to lead you. Your marriage will impact many lives."

Ha! Some impact. Was I content to be a "perfect example" of submission to God only in front of hundreds of people in my wedding dress? Or would I strive to be His servant and obedient child in my kitchen too?

I'm Never Coming Out!

"I had a real temper when your dad and I were first married," my mom told me recently.

"Good," I thought. "Now I have someone to blame for mine!"

"When I found out I was pregnant with you," she said, "your dad told the guys at work before I had a chance to tell anyone else."

Dad had casually mentioned the fact to Mom over supper that evening.

"I got so angry," Mom told me, "that I threw my hot dog at the front door! There was mustard everywhere. Your dad calmly walked over, wiped the mustard off the door with his fingers, licked them, picked the hot dog up off the floor, sat back down at the table, and ate it!"

I am proud to say that I have never thrown a hot dog at anyone, but I'm ashamed to admit how angry I used to get at Gabe. I'd scream hateful things at him right before I locked myself in the bathroom and refused to give in to his pleas from the hallway. He seemed to bring out the worst in me.

"When I start feeling backed into a corner," Joanne Heim says, "I lash out. I say mean, hurtful and ugly things that I end up regretting. When we were first married, this usually involved me throwing up my hands and heading for the bathroom where I'd lock the door and ignore Toben's knocking."[1] (Did she read my journal?)

You're smiling and thinking of your own childish behavior, aren't you? I haven't done the lock-myself-in-the-loo routine for quite a while. (Our bathroom door doesn't even have a doorknob at the moment—darn it.) But I still have my angry, jerky moments.

Just last month, Gabe and I got into it, and I was determined to convey my anger without using dirty or spiteful words.

"I...hate you...right now!" I blurted at one point in our heated conversation.

"You hate me right now?" he smirked. "You hate me *right now?*"

"That's what I said," I huffed stubbornly.

"You hate me right now. Well, that's nice. Are you going to write that in your little marriage book?"

It drives me nuts when he throws this book in my face—and he knows it.

"Oh, Gabe is so wonderful," he gushed, mockingly. "I love him sooo much...I hate you right now...Gabe is my dream husband...I hate you right now..."

"Shut up!" I yelled. "I get your point!"

How do you deal with arguments? The Heims suggest that we should never bring up the past, exaggerate, intimidate, give up, refuse to talk, humiliate, change the subject, or interrupt.[2]

Sorry to be a party pooper, but if you're regularly incorporating these no-no's into your marital conflict resolution, it's time to pull the plug.

Speaking in Anger

"It took many years," one woman told me, "before I learned to control my anger." Another friend of mine told me that she and her husband are still working on "talking things out without getting emotionally heated."

So how do we keep from exploding in anger when we're in the middle of a "lively discussion"?

One thing we can do is "bring up problems as they occur instead of letting them build," a friend of mine suggests. The longer we allow a problem to boil and steam below the surface, the greater the explosion will be when it finally gets aired out. Discussing issues as they come up can alleviate some of that pressure.

My friend Hailey and her husband have been focusing on that very thing in their new marriage. "We're always working on communicating and getting concerns out in the open before they get held in too long," she says. "That just leads to a big fight that we could have avoided."

One rule of thumb is to never say something in the middle of an argument that you wouldn't say in a normal conversation. "I hate you right now!" is one such example. Just because something is true doesn't mean we need to say it, especially if it's cruel.

Before opening your mouth to say anything, ask the Holy Spirit for self-control. Pray that you won't lash out in anger but will speak in kindness and love, even if that's the last thing on earth you feel like doing.

I'm reminded of a woman who had surgery on her vocal chords. She was unable to speak for weeks and had to communicate by writing on paper. When she was frustrated or angry with her husband or kids, she scribbled furiously on the tablet. But when she saw her nasty words written out on paper, she was aghast and ripped the paper to shreds.

What if we had to write all our words down before we said them to our husbands? Would that change our speech patterns just a bit?

Eating My Words

My daughters were napping, and I was eagerly anticipating an hour of uninterrupted work on this book.

Gabe came in from his office and sprawled out on the couch across from me. "I'm just going to take a quick nap," he said.

Great, I thought. So much for peace and quiet.

"Oh, I forgot to tell you..." Gabe said.

My eyes rolled at my computer screen. "Yes?" I swiveled my body around in my chair. (My chair, unfortunately, does not swivel.) The swiveling motion made my neck hurt, on top of the headache I already had. I was annoyed. I half-listened to him, making my annoyance obvious, then turned back to my keyboard.

"Oh, and..."

I turned around again, irritation spreading across my face like chicken pox.

"Yes?"

More talking. Blah, blah, blah. If only he would go away. Finally, he finished. I turned back around, my fingers poised to strike the keys.

"What are you writing?" he had the audacity to ask.

That was it.

"Okay," I said. "Can we just get one thing clear? I came out here to write. I thought you were going to take a nap. Stop talking and let me work!"

"I just asked what you were doing."

"I'm *writing!*"

"Writing what?"

Before the words escaped my lips, I knew I was in trouble. "My marriage book," I said, lowering my gaze.

Purely out of guilt, I walked over to the couch and hugged him. "I'm sorry. I have a headache, and I'm taking it out on you."

"Could you do me a favor," he asked, "and stop taking everything out on me? Then you wouldn't have to apologize all the time."

"Oh, and you never take anything out on me. Is that it?"

A fight ensued. What else was new? These fights are all the same. It's discouraging. I'm running out of patience with myself. Why can't I just be a good wife and get on with my life? Why do I keep messing up? Who am I to be writing a book about marriage when I can't even follow my own brilliant advice?

Yet I will continue to write, being inspired by some words of Paul's I read yesterday:

> I'm not saying that I have this all together, that I have it made. But I am well on my way, reaching out for Christ, who has so wondrously reached out for me. Friends, don't get me wrong: By no means do I count myself an expert in all of this, but I've got my eye on the goal, where God is beckoning us onward—to Jesus. I'm off and running, and I'm not turning back (Philippians 3:12-14 MSG).

"When I look back at the times that I have argued or become angry with someone," one woman shared with me, "it is almost always because I was thinking of myself."

I had taken my focus off Christ and centered instead on my own selfish desires. Back to the drawing board. Again.

Fighting Smartly

How you say things during an argument is important. Delivering your message in a calm manner will make a more effective statement than lashing out in a hateful barrage of spiteful words.

Setting should be considered as well. A public place is never a good environment for a "discussion." Don't fight in front of friends or family members. Hurts inflicted during the argument are that much more painful when others witness the whole event.

Don't underestimate the importance of timing either. You've got to know your husband well to get the whole timing thing down. What kind of day has he had? What else is he dealing with right now? At what time of day is he generally most calm?

Over the years, I've learned to wait until Gabe is in a good mood, relaxed, and smiling to bring up something that might make waves. In the early years, I never took into consideration that "now might not be the best time."

The timing issue is crucial for *me* as well. When I'm suffering from PMS, I have no business bringing up issues that might lead to heated arguments. In my heightened hormonal state, I'll make mountain ranges out of anthills.

Fighting isn't all bad, if you do it right. Tension can be a good thing. Weightlifters need tension and resistance if they ever hope to build their muscles. Tension can strengthen our marriages too if we handle it correctly.

Here's to big, strong marital muscles!

Four Big Fight-Igniters

I read once that the four biggest things married couples argue about are money, sex, his mother, and her mother. Apparently it's true because those four showed up in my surveys more frequently than anything else.

"What do you argue about most these days?" I asked. "Money and sex," one woman told me. "My mother-in-law," another said. "Mothers—mine and his," said a third.

If you frequently argue about any of these four big issues, join the club! What else gets your fighting juices boiling?

"Intimate time together."

"Things that need to be done around the house."

"All the practical questions he asks when I want to buy something fun."

"Time management and priorities."

"Mike not wanting to visit my family as often as I want to."

"His new job getting finalized."

"We don't have enough time for each other—not like when you're dating."

"Money, chores, food (not having enough and Matt eating too much)."

"Me fussing at Paul for watching TV and not talking to me more."

"Him feeling that his hours spent at work are unappreciated and me feeling that my hard work around the house is unappreciated."

So much to fight about. So little time. How will you ever get all these issues resolved? One thing I've learned when I have too much to do and too few hours in my day is that I have to let some of it go. Give it up. Surrender.

Just Let Go

I've always been a sympathetic person—toward myself, that is! Gabe says the wrong thing at the wrong time, and tears form in my eyes and out come the balloons and streamers. I throw a good pity party.

In days past, I would rehash his words over and over and relish the pain that filled my chest. Poor, poor little me, with such heavy burdens to bear.

I don't remember exactly when it was, but at one point I decided

I needed to outgrow those little fiestas—and fast. I came up with a plan. When Gabe said something that hurt my feelings, I would recite the words "no self-pity" over and over to myself until the pain was gone. Sounds stupid, no? But it worked! After five or six repetitions, I forgot the offense and moved on.

"Gabe bit my head off today," I wrote in a journal entry dated March twelfth. "And I did not deserve it. My eyes began to tear up, and I was ready to dive headfirst into a pity puddle and wallow.

"However, I forced myself—and it was sooooo hard!—to mouth my new mantra—'no self-pity.' I wanted to quit right there, knowing for certain it was not going to work this time around. But I did it, and—sure enough—after just four reps, I was over it.

"I wanted so badly to throw those stupid little words out the window. Giving up self-pity is like giving up chocolate—comfort food! I just wanted to throw myself into self-pity's arms and burrow my head into her billowing bosom."

I once read about a woman who had her own interesting method of letting go. She designated a window of time in the future (say, Wednesday at 2:15) where she could hold a small pity party for herself. By the time her party was scheduled to begin, she had already forgiven and forgotten the offense.

Fights on the Road

What is it about riding in a car? Gabe and I have gotten into some nice-sized fights on our way to and from just about everywhere—church, the grocery, our parents' homes, ball games, even "hot" dates.

I can remember walking into a restaurant or movie theater on what was supposed to be a romantic evening away, wiping away tears of hurt and frustration and not speaking to Gabe for the next 15 minutes or even the rest of the night.

What's the big problem with a simple car ride? I don't have the answer, but I do have a few unproven theories. Maybe we know the other person has nowhere to run, and we use the drive time to ambush him. Maybe we're already rushed and stressed, trying to get somewhere on time, so any discussion we have inevitably escalates out of proportion. Maybe, like a friend of mine, fearing for your life puts you on edge. She literally dreads riding in the car with her husband.

"We argue all the time on the road," she says. "I'm terrified of his driving, so I'm already uptight and hanging on for dear life as he flies around curves, and then the fighting begins. It never fails. We can't even make it to church without arguing, and it's only a mile away!"

Just a month after my sister got married, my mom and I met her and her new husband at Subway, picked up subs for lunch, and drove separately to the park to eat—me with Mom, and Bethany with Stewart.

As we got out of our cars at the park, I caught Bethany taking a quick swipe across her red-rimmed eyes. She smiled and tried to act like her cheery self as we sat down at picnic tables to eat, but she wasn't fooling anyone. Things had been fine at Subway, so the fight had to have occurred during the five-minute drive to the park.

I casually hugged her and silently empathized with her predicament, remembering back to that same scene that seemed to recur with disconcerting frequency in my own first year of marriage. At the same time, I felt relief that I had been married six-and-a-half years, not six-and-a-half weeks.

Just last week, my cousin Brian eavesdropped on an interview (for this book) with some of my female relatives at a family get-together.

"Fighting in the car?" he said. "I've got some advice about that."

"Well, Brian, this book is written *by* women *for* women," I said with a smile, "but sure, go ahead. It couldn't hurt to hear a guy's perspective."

"If you're in a fight in the car, whatever you do, do not get out of the car," he warned, in all seriousness. "Especially if you're three miles from home and it's the dead of winter. And there are snow drifts piled high on either side of the road, and traffic is zooming by at least 40 miles an hour, if not faster. Definitely not a walking zone."

He was on a roll. "And your wife doesn't come back. You're three miles from home. In the bitter cold. On a busy road, walking three miles to get to your warm home and your lovely wife. The wife who left you stranded on the side of the road."

I wish you could have seen Brian telling his pitiful tale. Three years later, he still hadn't gotten over Christy leaving him alone in the snow. *Three miles from home.*

When he finally got home, he learned that Christy *had* come back. Not to pick him up and take him home, but to make sure he was okay. She drove right by him undetected and then went back home and waited for him to arrive. I love it.

"So what was your fight about in the first place?" I asked him when he finally finished his tale.

"Um...I can't exactly remember," he said. "Something about cookie dough."

The Thrill of the Fight

Speaking of arguments that are completely not worth it, I used to argue with Gabe just for the sake of arguing. It was some sort of thrill ride or power trip for me to think of snappy comebacks and biting retorts and use them to ultimately emerge the victor.

Do you have to get in the last verbal jab when you're fighting with your husband? I'm forever biting my tongue, straining to refrain from saying the last nasty word. Winning an argument might feel good for a moment, but it eventually leaves us empty inside. Marriage is not a game. It is not a sport. It is a relationship. If someone is winning in your marriage, you're both big fat losers.

Toben Heim refers to something he calls the "zero-sum game" we love to play. "Win/win means we both win," he points out. "In the zero-sum game, I don't care if I lose as long as you lose, too."[3]

Sometimes it helps to ask myself a simple question—"If I knew I were going to heaven tomorrow, would I still argue about this today?" When I look at life in light of eternity, most arguments are nothing short of petty.

He Who Is Forgiven Much…

Martin Luther once said that "a happy marriage is the union of two good forgivers." An opportunity comes up at least a couple times a day for me to forgive my husband, so I might as well get good at it.

But let's not forget how many times a day our husbands have to extend forgiveness to *us*. I sometimes think I could fill an entire page with Gabe's offenses, mistakes, and faults, but I casually overlook the six pages chronicling my own mess ups. That's called looking at the little speck in my husband's eye without noticing the two-by-four sticking out of my own face.

Do you expect your husband to be too perfect? Do you let him mess up once or twice or six times a day, or are you on his case for every little offense? What if you had to be as perfect as you expect him to be? Could you do it?

Psalm 103 speaks of God's unbelievable love and forgiveness toward us. Verse 10 says, "He does not treat us as our sins deserve or repay us according to our iniquities." I'm often guilty of both treating Gabe as I feel his sins deserve *and* repaying him according to his iniquities.

How would my marriage change if I followed God's example of

forgiveness and grace? Only by grace are my sins forgiven. Can I offer the same grace to Gabe?

I think of the story in Luke 7 of the sinful woman who bathed Jesus' feet with her tears and expensive perfume as He dined at the home of Simon the Pharisee. Simon was appalled that Jesus was letting such a despicable woman touch Him.

Jesus took the opportunity to share a story about two men who had been forgiven a debt by a moneylender—one owed 500 denarii, the other 50. Who loved that moneylender more? The one who had been forgiven the biggest debt, of course.

Jesus goes on to put Simon in his place. "Do you see this woman? I came into your house. You did not give me any water for my feet, but she…has not stopped kissing my feet…Therefore, I tell you, her many sins have been forgiven—for she loved much. But he who has been forgiven little loves little" (verses 44-47).

Imagine how much love your husband will have for you as you forgive him again and again, for small offenses and great.

When we withhold forgiveness from our husbands, either we don't realize the extent of the forgiveness we received when Christ died for our sins, or we don't appreciate it.

Maybe, Just Maybe, He's Right

When you're in the middle of an argument with your hubby, stop for a moment and put yourself in his shoes. Why does he feel this way? What am I missing here? Why does he object so strongly to my point of view? Are my motives pure or selfish?

If possible, drop the argument for a while and take time to pray. Don't ask God to change your husband's mind—as I used to do! Ask God to help you see the situation through His eyes. Ask Him to show you how to reach the solution that would be most pleasing to Him.

Just four days ago, Gabe and I had a huge argument. Ironically, we were driving home from the first night of a two-day marriage conference. We argued from the conference to the restaurant, all through our meal, and from the restaurant until we arrived home. We crawled into bed at midnight, exhausted.

I cried myself to sleep, praying over and over, "God, help me!"

Here's a brief synopsis of our fight. Long ago, my mom graduated from college with a teaching degree, taught for two years, had kids, and hasn't worked since. I was on the same track, more or less—except for the writing I did on the side. One of my sisters was months away from graduation and a wedding. The other sister was in her freshman year of college without a declared major.

My dad busts his rear end to pay off school bills, among other things, and Gabe's opinion is that a costly Christian college education is not worth the money for someone who ultimately wants to stay home and raise a family. We have two little girls who will grow up someday and potentially cost Gabe a lot of money.

Bottom line? I was hurt and offended by everything Gabe said about my family. I thought he was being insensitive, unfair, and unreasonable. As I cried out to God, I saw no solution in sight.

I woke up the next morning, feeling as if I had been flattened by a semi. I squinted at myself in the bathroom mirror and pow!—God spoke to me.

"Gabe's right," He said inaudibly but crystal clear.

What!

"Most of what he said was valid and true. His concerns are real and important. Much of what you said was selfish. Go tell him you've had a change of heart."

No kidding. This is what happened.

I took my shower, got dressed, and woke Gabe up with, "Hey, do you want to hear something exciting?"

I relayed God's message, and he smiled sleepily.

The moral of the story is that when two people argue, both of them usually think they're right. Certain arguments seem to be perpetual in our marriage. We can't agree, regardless of how many times we hammer it out.

The only solution is to take it to God. Ask Him to change your heart or your husband's, whichever He deems best. If you are fortunate enough to be the right one, ask God to show that to your husband. It works better that way. God reveals the truth to him *gently* rather than beating him over the head with it.

In my case, I'm often the one who gets reprimanded by God. He shows me the error of my thinking when I thought I could not have possibly been wrong.

An argument is productive when the conflict is resolved—or at least diminished—and you develop a better understanding of each other's point of view.

Thankfully, that's what happened with us that round.

And the Sun Goes Down

"Don't let the sun go down on your anger." That's not just a cliché—it's actually from the Bible (Ephesians 4:26 NASB). But you can interpret it in various ways.

If you take it literally, you won't let your head hit the pillow at night after a fight with your husband until you're no longer mad at him. In other words, you could be up all night. And all day. And the next night.

I personally don't think you have to solve every conflict before you go to sleep. I do think it's best to look at each other and say, "We still haven't reached a conclusion. I still think you're wrong. But I'm determined not to go to bed hating you. I want a kiss, a hug, and a promise that we can continue this discussion tomorrow, after we've each had a good night's sleep and a chance to calm down and consider each other's perspective."

Things always seem brighter in the morning. If it's getting late and you're still fighting, your chances of solving your problem keep getting slimmer. And technically, the sun probably went down hours before.

Put the issue aside for a short time and try again when you have more energy and a fresh outlook on things. Sleeping on it really can help. The important thing is—and I believe it's the point of the sun-anger verse—we should be quick to offer forgiveness. A grudge brings nothing but grief—particularly to the one holding it.

Your Hubby's Not the Enemy

Marriage is a picture of Christ and the church. Satan can't destroy Christ, so he would like nothing more than to destroy our marriages. When we aren't in unity with our husbands, Satan gets a foothold.

Think of the game red rover, where one team holds hands at one end of the field and calls over a member of the other team. "Red rover! Red rover! Send Susie right over!" The goal is to hold hands so tightly that the opponent can't break through. We need to be gripping our husbands' hands so tightly that Satan can't break our hold.

Believe me, he never stops trying. There's no room for error, no time to take a break from unity for a while. Mark 3:25 reads, "If a house is divided against itself, that house cannot stand."

Your husband is not the enemy; Satan is. Remember that the next time you're tempted to battle your mate.

Part Three

Treating Hubby God's Way

5

Submission...Seriously?

Wives, submit to your husbands as to the Lord.
For the husband is the head of the wife as Christ is the
head of the church…as the church submits to Christ,
so also wives should submit to their husbands in everything.

EPHESIANS 5:22-24

"I didn't get married so some man could tell me what to do!"

"Submission? Are you serious? This is the twenty-first century!"

"My husband is *not* the boss of me!"

"If anybody wears the pants in this family, it's gonna be me!"

Try wandering down a crowded city street and randomly pulling women aside, asking them to define "submission to your husband." You'll be lucky to get much more than dirty looks and a smattering of filthy words.

Even Christian women balk at the idea. Before I was married, I attended a wedding at my church. At the reception, a woman walked up to me, shaking her head from side to side.

"That was a nice ceremony," she noted. "Except for all that stuff about submission. I didn't think there were any preachers left who still talked about that nonsense." The pastor's words had come straight from the Bible—Ephesians 5. Is that all God's Word is—nonsense?

When we think of submission, we often picture a doormat, with others—our husbands in particular—bossing us around and walking all over us. Keeping our mouths shut and our opinions to ourselves. Is that what God had in mind?

Peter, Paul, and Mary

Let's back up a couple thousand years. In Jesus' day, women were insignificant, valued less than property or animals. Their opinions didn't matter. They weren't good for much at all besides cooking, cleaning, and making babies—preferably boy babies. They were disposable, dispensable, and degraded by men.

Enter King Jesus. Jesus brought women up from their lowly positions to a place of honor. He gave them significant roles to play in His earthly ministry and treated them with utmost respect. He spoke to them with kindness and love. Even the lowliest of the lowly—like the formerly demon-possessed Mary Magdalene and the adulterous woman at the well.

So where have we gotten the idea that Jesus was out to subjugate women into submission to domineering men? In reality, Jesus did more for the women's lib movement than anyone else in history.

"So maybe *Jesus* loved women," you're thinking, "but what about Peter and Paul? They're the ones who wrote all that submission stuff in the Bible."

We need to realize that these guys weren't questioning or denouncing a woman's worth. They were followers of the Master, and just like Jesus, they respected and honored women. Women played key roles in both Peter's and Paul's ministries in the early church.

Paul writes in Galatians 3:27-28, "For all of you who were baptized into Christ have clothed yourself with Christ. There is neither Jew nor Greek, slave nor free, *male nor female,* for you are all one in Christ Jesus" (emphasis added). No one is a second-class citizen in God's kingdom.

Peter (not to be confused with the pumpkin eater who kept his wife in a pumpkin shell—now there's a pig for you!) tells husbands in 1 Peter 3:7 to show honor and respect to their wives as fellow heirs with them of God's grace.

A common Jewish daily prayer in Paul's day said, "I thank my Lord that I am not a Gentile or a woman." In Paul and Peter's age and culture, people did not commonly respect women in any fashion. In a radical departure from the status quo, Paul and Peter showed women the respect and esteem they rarely got from the rest of the population.

With divine inspiration, these apostles have shared with us principles for marriage that God, the Creator of marriage, knows will work. If the word *submission* makes us cringe, we don't understand its full meaning.

Submission Is Not...

Perhaps the best way to tackle our concerns about submission is to first spell out what submission *doesn't* mean, Dale Burke suggests. He offers these helpful clarifications:

Submission does not mean you're inferior to your husband. The Bible tells us that Jesus submitted to God, His Father. Jesus wasn't inferior to God. He *is* God. In the Bible, the person doing the submitting is never in an inferior position.

Submission does not mean keeping your mouth shut. We're not condemned to suffer in silence when our husbands fail to lead us and love us as Christ does. First Peter 3:1-2 does tell us that husbands may be "won over without words" by the Christlike behavior of their wives. But surely this means to stop *nagging,* not "don't ever open your mouth."

Submission does not mean rolling over and playing dead. The verb *submit* is active, not passive. It's something you *do,* not something that is done *to* you. It's something you give as a gift to someone else, not something that he or she demands of you.

Submission does not mean rolling over and playing dumb. We don't blindly submit to our husbands' leadership. Submission is an informed, intelligent, thoughtful decision. This isn't a case of the dumber submitting to the smarter. In many cases, the wife may have wisdom equal to or superior to her husband's. (No, this is not the time for a hearty "amen.") You *choose* to follow your husband's leadership—with all your brain cells firmly intact.

"Submitting…should never relegate a woman to just sitting on the bench," Burke says. "She was not designed by her Creator to be the team water girl, waiting to spring to action during time-outs and intermissions. She is more like a valued assistant coach, serving alongside the head coach for life."[1]

God's Plan for Submission

Our first priority is to submit ourselves to God. Christ submitted to His Father when He "made himself nothing, taking the very nature of a servant" and prayed that God's will be done in His life regardless of the cost (Philippians 2:7).

"God's power is too precious and powerful," Stormie Omartian says, "to be let loose in an unsubmitted soul."[2] I don't want to miss out on God's power because I'm too big to submit.

After we submit ourselves to God, we submit to the people He has placed in authority over us. "Everyone must submit himself to the governing authorities," Paul writes, "for there is no authority except that which God has established" (Romans 13:1). These guys were pagan Roman leaders—not godly men—so this verse still applies today when we have godless leaders governing us.

That said, what do we do when someone asks us to violate God's commands? First Peter 3:1 challenges us to submit to our husbands even if *they* don't obey God. But we certainly shouldn't obey a man who tells *us* to disobey God. In Acts 5:29, when the Jewish authorities told the apostles to quit teaching in Jesus' name, the apostles refused, saying, "We must obey God rather than men."

Wives are to submit to their husbands *as to* the Lord—not *instead of* the Lord. If your husband asks you to do something that explicitly contradicts God's Word, don't do it. Pray for strength, respectfully decline, and explain why. This won't be easy. If you're ever confronted with abuse because of your stand, don't sit there and take it. Get help!

Order in the Court

Many say that submission doesn't apply to us today, but 1 Corinthians 11:3 says, "The head of every man is Christ, and the head of the woman is man, and the head of Christ is God." God's Word says what it says, and like it or not, it still holds true.

All of us submit to authority. When we're on the road, we submit to the police. In court, it's the judge. When we pay taxes each April, the IRS. At work, it's your boss. In school, your teacher or professor.

Even talk show panels have one person chosen as the moderator or discussion leader, like Meredith Vieira on *The View.* Meredith isn't superior to her peers. Her job is merely to keep the scheduled topics on track, to keep the conversation orderly and under control. Otherwise, everyone would end up talking all at once, no one would hear what anyone else was trying to say, half the topics would go uncovered, and the show would quickly be taken off the air.

What would happen if no one were required to submit to anyone in any situation? Chaos at the least, disaster and devastation most likely. The God of decency and order has a master plan for His world to run smoothly. A key part of that plan is for us to submit to whatever authority He has placed over us in any given situation.

Anyone who has served in the army knows that rank has nothing to do with your value as a person. It has to do solely with order and authority. Without ranks, the army would be in an utter state of confusion. Try winning a war when no one knows who makes the decisions! You might as well just shoot yourselves.

Does God look at you as a person and see that you are inferior to your boss, your professor, your sergeant, or the local IRS agent? Of course not. We are all equal in God's sight. We submit to others' authority when they assume certain roles.

At a church picnic, if a policeman orders you to fill his plate with food, are you required to obey? No, at a church picnic, he's on equal footing with you. Kindly tell him to get his own sloppy joes.

Your husband is not superior to you—God created you equally. When God created Eve, He called her Adam's helper. The same word is used to describe God Himself. For someone to help you, that person has to be different from you, to have strengths you don't possess. A husband and wife bring different skills and gifts, opinions and personalities to the relationship. God created us to complement each other, not function independently. We're equal but not the same.

However, the role God placed your husband in is one of authority over you. In every area of life, someone plays the role of the authority figure. In marriage, God chose the husband to play this role.

Ideally (I love that word) your husband will love you as Christ loved the church. He gave His life for her. Who wouldn't be willing to submit to a lover like that? The only catch is that your husband will never be perfect like Christ. His love for you will never measure up to Christ's. Sometimes, it won't even come close.

Ideally...

The summer before I went to college, I worked in a motorcycle plant. Some of my coworkers gave me a hard time about being a

Christian, bringing up different topics to try to get me to doubt my faith. God was gracious in giving me answers, and occasionally I felt as if I actually made an impact.

One day the subject was submission. "So do you believe in that submission stuff?" they wanted to know. "You know, letting your husband boss you around and tell you what to do?"

"If my husband loves me," I told them smugly, "he'll have my best interests at heart, and submission will be no problem!" Of course, being single with no experience with marriage or submission, it all sounded so simple. He loves me and treats me like a queen. I submit. What's the problem?

I soon found out what the problem might be. My quick and easy submission formula that I swore by as a single girl didn't work out so well after I got married. My husband loved me, but did he always have my best interests at heart? Was he unselfish and loving at all times? Did he uphold his end of the Ephesians 5 bargain? Would I still submit when my human husband failed me?

Ideally, yes, it is a two-way street. But as tough as it is, God expects me to obey Him regardless of what my husband does. Nowhere in the Bible am I given permission to forsake my role if my hubby messes up in his.

"I won't submit to him until he starts loving me as Christ loves the church," Wife says.

"I'm not going to love her how she wants to be loved until she starts submitting to me as Christ submitted to God," says Husband.

Somebody has to go first! Let it be you! You're not a wimp for giving in. You're showing your strength by having the guts to make the first move.

We're all about fighting for our rights and looking out for number one. Jesus? Not so much. He wasn't a pushover or a weakling. And He didn't sit on His hands when people He loved were treated unfairly or God was being mocked. But He willingly submitted to His Father even when it meant sure death.

When It's Tough

"Submission is easy for *you*," one woman might say to another. "*Your* husband is kind and considerate. *My* husband is a real jerk, always rubbing submission in my face."

I know some women whose husbands are downright awful. Is it fair or practical to ask them to submit to an ungrateful, uncaring, selfish husband? It's not the least bit fair or practical—just biblical. Our obedience to the Lord isn't contingent on our husbands' behavior—it's not optional.

You may be thinking, "Who does she think she is, telling me how to live with my husband? She has no stinking idea what a *hard* marriage is really like." I'll concede to you on that point.

I can sympathize with you but not empathize. I have never personally experienced the anguish some of you have. I will say only one thing in my defense. I could share some things about my husband that would help us relate to each other more. But I want to honor him, not air his dirty laundry. What's past is past.

Maybe you would benefit more from a book written by someone in shoes closer to your size, so to speak. I do think, however, that the advice I've shared transcends all situations because it comes straight from God's Word.

First of all, you can save yourself a lifetime of heartache by marrying a believer. I once heard a preacher say, "If you don't marry a Christian, the devil will be your father-in-law." If God is not your husband's Father, then essentially, the devil is in that role. You're offering up an open invitation for Satan to make himself at home in your life and marriage.

A lot of women who find themselves in tough situations could have prevented the whole mess by not marrying the guy. Unless your marriage was arranged, you picked out your own husband. Anyone who knowingly marries an unbeliever—regardless of how nice he is—is asking for trouble. But it's not the end of the world. With lots of love and prayer and sacrifice, unsaved hubbies *can* be won to the Lord.

Some of us married men we knew weren't saved, thinking they would get saved sometime in the near future. Some of us married men with violent tempers, a propensity toward drunkenness, or complete disinterest in all things spiritual, but we hoped that would change. Very few of us walked down the aisle convinced we were marrying the world's godliest man—only to find out that he was a modern-day Jekyll and Hyde.

In my case, my husband was a believer, but for the first few years, his lack of spiritual leadership caused much grief and heartache. I contributed to the problem by trying to "fix" him the only way I knew how. Only recently has he begun to step up and assume his position as spiritual head of our family.

"As soon as Gabe gets his act together, I'll be a submissive wife," I used to think. Yet Jesus died on the cross for a world full of people who, to put it mildly, didn't have their act together. Jesus made the first move for us. Can we do that for our husbands?

The Freedom of Submission

Freedom and *submission* don't appear to be complementary terms. If you choose to submit, you give up your freedom. If you love your freedom, you can't submit. Right?

Wrong. Just as kids feel safe when they have clear boundaries and authority in place over them, we feel safe when our husbands are heads of our homes. Even though kids complain about rules and their parents not being fair, if they're completely honest, they crave these boundaries and rules.

We're the same way. We're God's kids, complaining because He made our husbands heads over us, and we don't think it's "fair." In actuality, we feel safe and secure—we don't have to worry about setting our own boundaries.

I think that's why some women marry jerks. We long for a man to step in and take on that leadership role. In our heart of hearts, we don't want to wear the pants in our marriages. Some of us just get confused between servant leadership and abusive control.

I noticed that freedom was a common theme when I asked women about submission. One friend of mine has been married to an unsaved man for more than 20 years, and even she finds submission freeing.

"It is a relief giving your husband the authority given by God for hard decisions," she says. "Sometimes I want to micromanage situations that are clearly my husband's department. When I give it up, I feel such a relief."

"I find great freedom being submissive to my husband," my friend Bea told me. "The more submissive I am, the more he loves me. The more he loves me, the more submissive I want to be."

"Submission takes an enormous load off of the wife," says my friend Wendy. "Women think it is limiting, but it is really freeing!"

Colleen agrees. "Besides being biblical (or maybe because it is), submission is very freeing. It frees me from manipulation, worry, and stress, and it frees up time to use my abilities productively."

"I am so grateful when my husband steps in and helps me realize I am overextending," one woman said. "I feel so protected because of his love and the way he expresses it to me by not allowing me to go beyond my limits."

Down deep, submission is what we really want. We want our husbands to take care of us, be responsible for us, protect us, and be held accountable for us. It takes all the pressure off. We have enough to worry about.

But we want to have our cake and eat it too. We want all the fringe benefits of a loving, protective husband, but we want the freedom to act however we want. Same with our Christian walk—we can't have all the blessings of following Christ and still walk the broad road of sin. The Bible says we'll either be slaves to sin or slaves to righteousness. We're free to choose our master. Will it be God or sin?

"I am not submitting to my husband!" we say. "That is so old-fashioned!" Yet we want our husbands to act in plenty of other old-fashioned ways. The flowers, the opened doors, the romance, the chivalry. Our deepest longings are old-fashioned.

We want to pick and choose the "traditional husband" roles our guys play. Nobody wants a wimpy man, but we don't want to be told what to do. We want spiritual leaders, but we don't want to submit to that leadership.

Lisa and Doug struggled with this issue in their marriage. Lisa considers herself a feminist but still longed for the image of man as protector. She soon realized that submission didn't mean giving up her freedom and identity.

"Lisa longed for Doug to be the spiritual head of their relationship and found a great deal of comfort in knowing that he would make the difficult decisions they faced. Because of that, Doug felt supported and empowered by Lisa and made decisions that were honoring to her."[3]

Submission has a flip side. The person who has the last say also has to deal with the responsibility for his decisions. Being the final authority of a household sounds great and all, but it's a tough job— one I'm more than willing to let my husband assume. Sure, it has its perks, but we can't have our cupcakes *and* lick off the icing.

While the principle of submission gives our husbands the bulk of the responsibility, we aren't off the hook by any stretch.

Romans 14:13 (MSG) tells us, "Forget about deciding what's right for each other. Here's what you need to be concerned about: that you don't get in the way of someone else, making life more difficult than it already is."

"Mike is accountable to the Lord for our family," my friend Colleen told me, "and I do not want to make his job more difficult. When I stand before Jesus Christ, I do not want Him to say that I made Mike's job hard."

Just as submitting is easier when your husband is a loving leader, *leading* is easier when others lovingly submit. Don't get in the way of God's will for your husband's life. Make his job as the head of your home a joy.

Let Him Lead

"Why won't Gabe be a spiritual leader?" I used to fuss and fume. "That's what Christian husbands are supposed to do."

Then one day I looked down at my hands and noticed that my fists were tightly clenched, my knuckles white. All these years I had been griping at Gabe for not taking the reins, and here I was, clutching them for all I was worth.

Janet knows what I mean. "Satan is so cunning about making me compromise and take up the reins if I think Paul isn't doing something fast enough," she says.

My mom did the same thing with my dad in the early years of their marriage. "I thought he would automatically take the leadership role once we were married," she told me, "but I take the blame for that because I wouldn't let him lead at first."

"To be honest, I don't think I've done very well with submission," one friend told me. "By nature, I'm very controlling, and I tend to be that way with our relationship."

I thought I knew what a spiritual leader looked like, and I expected Gabe to conform to that image, but I wasn't taking into account his personality, his gifts and abilities, his strengths and weaknesses, his likes and dislikes. I was comparing him to other men and didn't consider the fact that spiritual leadership can take different forms.

I would nag him to read his Bible more, ask him why he never initiated prayer time with me, and criticize him whenever he lost his temper or made an error in judgment. But all the nagging and criticizing had an adverse effect.

I was beginning to resemble a dictator, and Gabe wasn't about to risk usurping me. "Fine," he subconsciously thought. "If you don't trust me enough to lead, then I'm not doing *anything* you want me to do. No praying. No reading my Bible. Why bother?"

"You think I'm a failure, don't you?" I remember him asking me once. "Nothing I do is ever good enough." Ouch. He had received my not-so-subtle message loud and clear.

We want our husbands to be men and stand up and take charge, yet we balk and rebel any time they try to take a leadership role in our marriages. I don't enjoy having Gabe question my motives or hold me accountable for my words and actions. We want a spiritual leader, but we're not willing to submit to that leadership.

"I used to be very bossy," a friend confided, "and I wasn't happy. I've found I'm much more content when I let my husband lead."

"When I am willing to be submissive," another friend told me, "he is more willing to be a leader."

"Life would be a lot easier," one woman said, "if I would just submit and let my husband be in charge. When I am submitting, I am right where God wants me."

The Law of Rewards

Not a day goes by without a moment or two when I want to do anything but submit. Moments when it would feel so good to bite Gabe's head off and pay him back for something he said or did.

At those times, submission takes sheer willpower. I have to *force* myself to take the high road and do what's right. It takes everything I've got—and a good helping of grace from the Holy Spirit.

I never regret submitting. Instead of ten minutes of "pleasure" (self-pity and angry words), I get a lasting sense of peace and joy from doing what God has called me to do. If I can just convince myself to give up the temporary pleasures of sin, He always rewards me with something much greater.

The Bible tells us we'll be rewarded in heaven for obeying Christ on earth. But we don't always have to wait for eternity to reap the benefits of obedience. I asked women to share with me the rewards they've received as a result of submitting to their husbands.

"I can see in myself a more submissive spirit in every aspect of my life."

"A great marriage, and a great husband who loves to be home and with us."

"Protection, mainly. It is a very safe feeling."

"My husband's spiritual growth."

"Time to do my job, since I am not trying to do his job for him."

"A husband who loves me and leads us in what God wants us to do."

"A husband who values my opinion and will do anything for me."

"Peace and genuine contentment."

"Harmony and oneness with my husband."

"A fun and rewarding relationship with my husband and God."

"God answers prayer and takes care of things."

"My husband feels more like a man—he's fulfilling God's role for him."

"Witness to others observing our home."

These answers were very humbling to me—and encouraging. It's exciting to see what I have to look forward to when I trust God to help my husband lead our home.

What Submission Looks Like

Many of the women who have the hardest time with the passage in Ephesians 5 had parents who didn't live it out. Submitting to your husband is tough if your mom never modeled that to you when you were growing up. I was blessed to have a mom who submitted to my dad, but that didn't mean it was easy.

My friend Tari didn't have that privilege. Today Tari says she believes in the concept of submission 100 percent, but she didn't always feel that way. "I rarely had an opportunity to see it modeled before me," she says.

Tari's parents divorced when she was eight, and she was used to seeing a woman make all the decisions. During Tari's single years, the women's movement spoke out strongly against submission.

"For someone like me," she says, "who had not seen a model and had heard nothing but negative comments about it, I thought I knew all I needed to know."

Then something changed. "Once I began to study God's Word for myself," she says, "I began to see the lies that I'd believed. But even once you get your thoughts corrected, it's still difficult to live out the action."

So if you've never really seen submission in action, how are you going to know how to do it? What does it look like in the flesh, played out in your real-life marriage?

A lot of it is personal—between you and God (and your husband). I can give you some general guidelines, but you'll have to work out the details in your own marriage, using what you learn as you spend time talking to God and studying His Word.

In a nutshell, you shouldn't go against your husband if what he says doesn't contradict Scripture. Share your opinion, give your reasons, but let him make the final decision. Your part is to ask God to honor you for being submissive. He will.

My friend Pat told me, "My feelings on submission definitely changed as I grew in my relationship with God and my trust of Rick. Now I'm comfortable with discussing issues in private but letting Rick be the public spokesman for our family."

One woman said, "We are equal and should work together, but my husband has the last say if he differs in opinion."

My friend Sue put it this way, "Someone has to be the boss! God made the husband to be that. We can give our opinions and concerns and intuitions, but he has the final say. He is my equal and my loving leader as I submit to him."

Shari looks at submission in a wonderful light. "It is a joy and a privilege to be Tim's wife—not a doormat but surrendered to Christ and my husband."

What if being your husband's wife is not a joy or privilege? One woman said she's fine with submitting "as long as the submission is not because of your husband's laziness" while another woman admitted that "I just have a problem with the way I'm expected to do some things."

What about the negative, demeaning husband who never has anything nice to say? What about the bossy, controlling husband who demands that you serve him from sunup to sundown? "Bring me my slippers! Get me a drink! Where is my supper? Fetch me the mail! Clean up this house!"

Ask yourself this: What is the best way I can show the love of Jesus Christ to the man I married? Pray about it. Ask God to give you wisdom, and He will. This question has no easy answer. I wish it did.

Just remember—deep down inside, we don't really want to be the head of our homes. We long to fill a different role. I love what Stormie Omartian says: "Part of making a house a home is allowing your husband to be the head so you can be the heart."[4]

Submission and the Modern Woman

Married women today find themselves in a quandary. They balk at a traditional marriage but secretly long for so many of its elements. At first glance, many of the Bible's commands seem legalistic, chauvinistic, and outdated. But after ignoring those commands and doing things our own way, we realize that God's way has merit after all.

Many of my friends struggled initially with submission. "I used to really hate the subject," Patty admits, "until I did a Bible study on it. It is so misunderstood."

"It's not the cuss word I thought it was," April told me, "but it's a beautiful thing when you do it in a godly way."

"At first this was a major issue for me," one friend said, "because I am very strong-willed, and submission was not in my vocabulary. Now I have a whole different outlook. I'm learning to be submissive but still be myself."

The word *submission* is taboo among most non-Christian women in the twenty-first century. Writers rarely mention it—even with contempt—as if merely typing the word will invite the gods of feminism to swoop down and strike them dead. The general consensus is that women have come too far and worked too hard to be demeaned and degraded by that horrid word. It's so un-PC, it's practically a racial epithet.

I just read a book about marriage by a woman who doesn't know

Christ personally, and the more I read, the sadder I felt for her. She wanted so desperately to cling to her feminist beliefs yet still achieve ultimate happiness and success in her marriage, and she found those two worlds colliding time after time. She feared losing her identity in her husband, yet she longed to love him completely. She wanted her independence, yet she longed for the strong protector-husband.

The bottom line was that her mind was telling her how the world views love and marriage, and her heart was telling her how God created her to love and be loved. Ironically, many feminists have come to the conclusion on their own that true happiness in life comes only after giving something up for the one you love. Many things change with time, but God's commandments don't. Anyone who understands the biblical view of submission knows it isn't about greeting your husband at the door in your apron. Submission is an attitude—the attitude Christ Himself had toward His Father.

Once you wrap your mind around the concept of submission as God originally designed it—*wow!*—you have never known freedom like this.

6

R-E-S-P-E-C-T

And the wife must respect her husband.

EPHESIANS 5:33

What is the number one thing men want from their wives? Sex would be my guess, but according to a recent survey, the top answer given by husbands was *respect*. We all want respect, but it's especially important to guys.

What *is* respect? How do we show it? Does it have to be earned? What happens when respect is missing in a marriage? Good questions! I'm so glad you asked.

Men Crave Respect

At the end of Ephesians 5, Paul commands men to *love* their wives, yet he instructs women to *respect* their husbands. Why the difference in word choice? And whatever happened to submission?

Dale Burke says, "Respect is the real issue for men...The real target in God's sights is to see wives showering their husbands with a gentle rain of respect. It is the gift that best says to a man, 'I love you.'"[1]

God created women to crave love and men to hunger for respect and admiration. He knew what they wanted and needed 2000 years ago, and nothing has changed. God also instructed women to submit, but that's not what men desire most. Submission is a means to an end. Respect is that end.

119

Have you noticed that the male ego is fragile? People call women the weaker sex and define masculinity as roughness and toughness, but the male ego is surprisingly delicate. When your husband's ego suffers damage due to failure or embarrassment, he needs your support and encouragement. And he needs you to never, *ever* be the source of that embarrassment.

I don't think we have a clue how much control we have over our husbands' self-image. We really can make or break them.

"You don't know my husband," you argue. "He couldn't care less what I think about him. Every negative thing I say rolls right off his back."

To that, I say hmm…problem detected. If you're constantly saying, "You need to change this…fix this…you never…why are you always so…," no wonder your comments don't seem to have any effect! You've hurt him so deeply that his only defense mechanism against further pain is to shut you out completely. Your husband needs to know you respect him, believe in him, admire him, and trust him to make wise decisions!

"But I *don't* respect him," you say. "He's always messing things up!"

I'm going to get a little firm here because this is a lesson I learned the hard way. Hopefully I can spare you some grief.

When He Doesn't Deserve It

You've probably heard that respect is something you have to earn. I think we readily accept this as fact and are quick to apply it to our husbands. It certainly sounds plausible enough.

If by *respect,* we mean an intangible *feeling* of admiration and approval, then I agree with the assertion. Yes, respect must be earned. It's hard to command ourselves to *feel* a certain way about someone unconditionally.

But just as love is something you *do,* not something that you *feel,* respecting your husband is an action, not a feeling.

When you *feel* respect for your husband, showing it is easy. Your actions naturally flow from the feelings inside you. But God often calls us to do something more difficult—show our husbands respect when we *don't* feel it, when he *doesn't* deserve it.

One woman advised me to "respect your husband even if he hasn't given you any reason to. Each of us can work on becoming a more consistent, responsible, respectable person."

First Peter 2:17 exhorts us to "show proper respect to everyone." This includes your husband—faults, imperfections, and all. We don't always think of respect as a command, but it is. It's not something we may freely choose to give or withhold.

We are much more concerned—obsessed almost—that *we* be respected. "How dare he not give me the respect I deserve?" Never mind that at the same time, we're blind to our own obligation to show respect to everyone.

Gary Thomas points out that the more my husband's weaknesses become familiar to me, the harder it is for me to give him respect. But failing to show Gabe respect is a sign of my own spiritual immaturity. Thomas says that respect is "more than an inevitable pathway of marriage. Giving respect is an obligation, not a favor; it is an act of maturity, birthed in a profound understanding of God's good grace."[2]

Failing to respect my husband—even when he doesn't deserve it—means that *I* am spiritually immature? That hardly seems fair.

We might think that if we had a different husband, showing him respect would be easier. "Of course she respects *her* husband," we say with a huff. "What has he ever done to *her?* I'd like to see her try to respect *my* husband."

If you can't respect the husband you've got, you probably won't be able to respect any other husband you go out and find either. Most people who have been married multiple times will tell you that changing spouses never makes respect an easier task. If anything, it becomes more challenging with each new marriage.

Someday we'll answer to God for any lack of respect we have shown to our husbands. But it's never too late to start making positive changes in our marriages. Out of respect for our heavenly Father, we respect those He has placed in our lives—namely our hubbies.

Unconditionally

Loving unconditionally is easy when the conditions are good. The same goes for respect. I can *say* that my love and respect for Gabe is unconditional, but do my actions show it?

You know those clothing items on the clearance rack that say "As Is"? You buy them with the understanding that they are flawed, and you forfeit the right to return them for being defective. So it goes with unconditional love and respect for your husband. You go into marriage with the understanding that this man is flawed, yet you promise to love and respect him regardless.

When I begin to love Gabe "as is," he'll begin to feel confident in my love. Only then will changes come. They may be slow, but remember—God uses those slow-in-coming changes to produce patience in us wives!

The husband who doesn't feel unconditionally respected and accepted thinks (correctly) that you're trying to change him. It hurts his pride that you don't think he's good enough the way he is, and he's probably going to rebel.

I used to think, "If I accept him like this, he'll never see the need to change." Your husband, whoever he is, deserves a wife who will see him for who God made him to be, and who will love him unconditionally. Can your husband talk to you—honestly share his heart—without being ridiculed? If not, it's no wonder he won't talk.

A funny thing happens after we've been married for a while. We stop thinking about our husbands' needs and how we can meet them. Instead, we focus solely on what they can do for us. We dwell on their faults and failures as husbands, fathers, lovers, and providers. They can never measure up.

We nitpick and henpeck so much that our husbands can't even earn our respect if they try. Nothing is good enough for us. As if we're the queen of England.

Sometimes we're hurt by our husbands' lack of respect for us, so we lash out at them in return.

When my husband fails to respect me, I have two choices. I can work harder to earn his respect, or I can constantly tear him down in order to convince myself that his lack of respect for me doesn't matter—he must be a loser anyway.

Let's choose to be respectable people and show respect to our husbands no matter what.

A Lousy Example

Have you ever been around a woman who treats her husband like dirt, even in public? Early in our marriage, we knew a couple that served as a perfect example to us—of how not to treat each other. The problem was not actually the couple but the wife. Her lack of respect for her husband was appalling.

We sat at the same table at a church potluck once (and never again). The wife had to use the restroom but didn't want to lose her place in line, so she told her poor husband to fill up a plate for her. His horrified look said it all.

"Uh...I don't know what you like," he told her, obviously terror-stricken.

"Oh, *please,*" she said with a roll of her eyes. "You know what I like. I like what *you* like."

With a tortured look of pain and resignation, he set out to do her bidding. And as he came to each dish, I could read the anguish in his face. He made it through the line somehow and sat down at our table.

Upon her return, his wife unleashed a barrage of criticism and sarcastic, biting remarks.

"*Two* pieces of fried chicken? What do you think I am, a *cow?*"

"You didn't get me enough pasta salad to feed a *flea!* Thanks a lot!"

"Are these black olives? I *hate* black olives!"

"Marla has julienne potatoes (whatever those are)—why didn't you get *me* any?"

"Where's my dessert? You know all the good stuff will be gone by the time we're finished with our meal. For crying out loud!"

I was so embarrassed for the two of them that *I* wanted to cry out loud. Or crawl under the table. I have come to realize that the glaring sins we see in others are usually the ones we do battle with in our own lives. A disturbing thought. My disgust with her blatant disrespect signaled that I also have struggles in this area.

"Every time you criticize someone, you condemn yourself," Paul says. "It takes one to know one. Judgmental criticism of others is a well-known way of escaping detection in your own crimes and misdemeanors. But God isn't so easily diverted. He sees right through all such smoke screens and holds you to what *you've* done" (Romans 2:1-2 MSG).

Ouch. Those words slice right through my self-righteousness.

Disrespectful Bible Wives

David, king of Israel, was excited. The ark of the Lord was finally carried to Jerusalem, and the people were rejoicing. David was so full of joy that while the entire house of Israel was bringing up the ark of the Lord with shouts and trumpets, David, dressed in a linen ephod, "danced before the LORD with all his might" (2 Samuel 6:14).

I'm not exactly sure what a linen ephod looked like or what David's dance entailed, but "with all his might" suggests that he went all out—held nothing back.

As all this was transpiring, Michal, David's wife, was watching out a window. When she saw her husband "leaping and dancing before the LORD, she despised him in her heart."

When hubby comes home, Michal is unabashedly verbal about her lack of respect for him. "How the king of Israel has distinguished himself today," she says, her voice dripping with sarcasm, "disrobing in the sight of the slave girls of his servants as any vulgar fellow would!"

He calmly responds, "I will celebrate before the LORD," and then delivers one of my favorite David-lines—"I will become even more undignified than this."

Michal was overly concerned about her reputation, and her love for David was apparently conditional. As long as he made her look good, all was well. But if he did something that she saw as humiliating or undignified, she let him hear about it. As punishment for her disrespect, she had no children to the day of her death.

Another example of a disrespectful wife was Queen Vashti. Married to King Xerxes, "she was lovely to look at" (Esther 1:11). As she and her husband hosted elaborate banquets for the women and men of the kingdom, respectively, the king sent his attendants to retrieve the queen so the king could show her off.

She wasn't really in the mood to be paraded in front of a bunch of drunk and gawking men (can't say that I blame her, but that's not the point), so she refused to come.

The king wasn't quite sure how to handle this disrespect from his wife, so he looked to his nobles for advice. They warned him that if he didn't take drastic action, all the women in the kingdom would despise their husbands, and "there will be no end of disrespect and discord." Vashti's banishment was proclaimed throughout the vast realm so that "the women will respect their husbands, from the least to the greatest."

Sarah showed disrespect for Abraham by convincing him to go against God and sleep with her handmaiden. Rebekah disrespected Isaac by helping their son Jacob trick his brother Esau out of Isaac's blessing. Bathsheba showed a blatant disrespect toward Uriah by having an affair with another man—the king.

All of these women faced God's judgment for their sinful, disrespectful choices.

Hold Your Tongue

Hold on a second while I climb up on my soapbox. Okay, I'm up. Hey, nice view. The advice I'm about to give you is some of the most important you'll ever get. Ready?

Never, ever, ever say anything to your husband—or about him—in public that will hurt his ego or embarrass him in front of others. Never. It's bad enough to ridicule or criticize him in the privacy of your own home, but doing it in public is inexcusable. The damaging effects on your husband and your relationship will be long lasting.

Mitzie, a friend of mine who had been married less than a year, shared with me the subject of her first fight with her new husband. "It was me pointing out Mike's flaws to others," she says. "I know, I'm mean, but I thought it was funny at the time. I now know it definitely was not funny."

Mitzie is wise to have figured this out as soon as she did. Some women never figure it out, and even if they do, they don't care. A good laugh is worth more to them than their husbands' emotions.

I know the temptation of saying something that would bring the house down in laughter but would hurt your hubby's feelings. Make the right choice!

I sat watching Gabe play on his church softball team one night last summer. The opposing team was up to bat, and the fans were cheering for the batter. Then a lone voice broke out of the crowd.

"If you don't do something good, you're sleeping on the couch tonight!" yelled the man's wife. She had a flock of girlfriends around her who all began cackling at her "cute" remark.

I immediately turned to see her husband's reaction. He was trying to smile, but his face was morphing into a bold magenta hue. He was obviously embarrassed.

His wife might have thought she was being funny, but I failed to see the humor. The last thing a husband needs is for his wife to mock and harass him in public and insinuate that sex is something she only gives him as a reward when he earns it.

The tongue has been called the deadliest of all blunt instruments. James agrees, devoting a good portion of his five-chapter book to the tongue's power to destroy.

"Sticks and stones may break my bones, but words will never hurt me!" A sing-song rhyme that, as seven-year-olds, we spat back at those who poked "fun" at us.

Words *can* hurt us. Badly. Words are what we remember. They leave deeper scars than physical inflictions. Memories of hurtful words can engulf you years down the road, but the black eye you got in the fifth grade won't be such a painful recollection.

If you really want to hurt someone, embarrass him in front of other people. And the worst hurt comes from a spouse—someone who is supposed to love you more than anyone else does. The pain lingers far too long to make it worth the brief moment of satisfaction you might get. Most of the time, your searing conscience drains all the fun out of the moment anyway.

Keep your complaints and criticisms to yourself. Use your words to help others see your man in the best possible light. Choose your husband over a good laugh. You won't regret it.

Respect His God-Given Gender

The differences between men and women go much deeper than our outward appearances and reproductive parts. We think and feel differently as well. These differences are good ones. God designed us this way for a reason.

For example, I've learned that Gabe doesn't want to hear long, drawn out, detailed accounts of what I did all day. He likes simple stories, highlights, that sort of thing. Don't know what I mean? Watch *Sportscenter* on ESPN. Hours and hours of sports coverage all condensed down into a nice, flashy, concise little 60 minutes. Just the facts—the good stuff.

We women get irritated with our husbands when they seem to lack interest in sitting down to a gabfest with us, but that's not what men do. They are wired differently. Ever hear of the book *Men Are Clams, Women Are Crowbars?*

We can share our hearts and have true intimacy with our husbands, but they aren't into the chatty little details that our girlfriends eat up—that's why God gave us women friends.

I'm sure you can think of plenty of other male-female differences. Like a spacecraft heating up when it reenters the atmosphere, marriages can get uncomfortably heated when our differences create friction.

Yes, differences can cause tension, but they can also be healthy when we learn to live with them and even *appreciate* them, when we figure out how God wants us to use them to strengthen and not weaken our marriages.

Focus on the Good

It's a given—a guarantee—that your husband will disappoint you. He's going to mess up. He's going to sin. Even with the best of intentions, he won't attain perfection or hit the mark every time.

You still need to respect him. It's not optional. Don't focus on his faults, as tempting as that may be. Set your sights on all that is good about the man you married. If you can't find anything, you're not looking hard enough.

Philippians 4:8 says, "Finally, brothers, whatever is true, whatever is noble, whatever is right, whatever is pure, whatever is lovely, whatever is admirable—if anything is excellent or praiseworthy—think about such things."

Take inventory of your thoughts. What percentage of them are mean and ugly? When critical thoughts enter your mind, kick them out and invite new ones in their place. Don't underestimate the power of positive thinking. Meditate on your husband's good qualities.

Then let him know what you love about him. Thank him, praise him, encourage him. Whatever you do, don't cancel it all out by saying something negative.

What if someone told me, "Marla, I really like you. You are smart and funny, kind and generous, charming and brilliant. If only you weren't so ugly."

*Pop! Sssssss…*That's the sound of the balloon that was my self-image deflating into utter flatness. Every kind word vanished into thin air in the second it took to say "If only you weren't so ugly." I'll remember nothing else.

That's how it is with our husbands. If we think we can esteem and honor them and then offhandedly toss in one little jab about how they could be working more overtime to pay the bills—*boom*. All that praise and positive encouragement becomes pointless—wiped off the slate by a single critical remark.

I can't count how many perfectly good compliments I've wasted in this manner.

The Face of Respect

"How do I know whether I am respecting my husband enough?" you ask. "Give me an example." Some examples of *disrespect* might be more helpful.

Do you roll your eyes—either to your husband's face or behind his back?

Do you find yourself frowning disapprovingly any time he shares an idea with you?

Do you find a way to turn every conversation into an argument?

Do you lie to him or purposely withhold the truth?

Do you treat sex as something he can have only after he meets a list of standards?

Do you make fun of him in front of others, even if it's "only" your own family?

Do you ignore him or give him the cold shoulder or the silent treatment?

Do you make snide comments about qualities you feel he lacks?

Do you talk negatively about him to others behind his back?

Do you complain constantly about things he does or fails to do?[3]

How did you do? If you answered yes to two or three or all of the above, you've got your work cut out for you. We all struggle with giving our husbands the respect they need. Not the respect they *deserve* but the respect they *need*.

What does respect look like in the flesh? How about smiling and nodding your head while he talks to you? Or a big kiss and squeeze when he gets home from work?

Share only the good things about your husband with your mom and your coworkers. Give him your full attention when he's talking. Share an interest in his hobbies.

Write him encouraging notes and stick them in his wallet. Tell him you admire him and are proud of the way he provides for your family.

Encourage him to pursue his dreams and tell him you believe in him. Offer to scratch his back. Initiate sex.

Your marriage will take a delightful turn when you start showering your husband with respect.

Pinpointed Praise

There was once a teacher who had her students write down what they liked about each of their classmates—to foster feelings of camaraderie among them. The teacher painstakingly copied those sentiments and presented each child with a list of what everyone liked about him or her. When I tried this experiment with a class of third graders, their responses made me smile.

Some chose to compliment others on their actions. "I like Nate because he brings great show and tells." "I like Forbes because he gives good hugs."

Some commented on physical characteristics. "I like Hilary because she's double-jointed." "I like Melissa because her hair is orange."

Some liked their classmates for what they *were*. "I like Andrew because he's sociable." "I like Amanda because she's comforting."

Some liked their classmates for what they were *not*. "I like Rebecca because she is not a tattletale." "I like David because he never disturbs you."

Some enjoyed how their classmates related to them. "I like Joshua because he is short like me." "I like Laura because she thinks everything I say is funny."

This simple exercise made me stop and think about my marriage. Everyone loves to hear they're special. And we love specifics—when someone pinpoints exactly what he or she likes about us and why.

No one needs to hear your pinpointed praise more than your husband. Just as my students praised each other, I can praise Gabe for his actions, his physical characteristics, what he is, what he's not, and how he relates to me. Here's a start:

> I like Gabe because he enjoys helping others.
>
> I like Gabe's perfect teeth, broad shoulders, and twinkling eyes.
>
> I like Gabe because he's strong but kind.
>
> I like Gabe because he never puts me down.
>
> I like Gabe because he teaches me new things.

Praise for Husbands

I asked a few women to tell me some specific things they really appreciate about their husbands. I was impressed with their thoughtful compliments, especially considering that a few of these husbands aren't even Christians. I hope these gals shared these words of affirmation not just with me but with their hubbies as well.

> "He helps out around the house, compliments the dinners I prepare, cuddles with me, and treats me like I'm precious. He always touches me to let me know I'm loved."
>
> "He is a good 'nurse' when I'm sick or not feeling well."
>
> "He kisses me just to let me know he's thinking of me, especially around other people. He reminds me that

I'm safe with him and that our friendship is strong even amid the chaos and regardless of my emotions or hormones."

"My husband is the least moody person I know. It is wonderful to know exactly what to expect from him every day. He is also the least judgmental person I know."

"He's not a workaholic, he doesn't try to make me do things I don't feel comfortable with, and he would rather spend time with me than friends."

"He's not really good about sharing his feelings verbally, but he'll do things he doesn't enjoy just to make me happy, like weed my flower bed, buy me candles, or go shopping."

"My husband is my best friend. We can share anything with each other."

"He is a wonderful Christian and has grown tremendously. It excites me even more to think of the man he will become."

"He is very sensitive to my needs. I feel very loved and supported at all times yet never smothered. I'm the best version of me because of my husband."

His Biggest Fan

Do you praise your husband often enough? Do you tell him what he means to you on a daily basis? Do you pinpoint certain things you appreciate? Are you satisfying his craving to be loved and admired?

If you're not fulfilling this basic need in your husband's life, he'll get it met somewhere else. It may be another woman. If you won't respect and encourage your husband, Satan has some pretty young thing waiting in the wings who will.

If you're not in the habit of being encouraging, ask God to help you start today. Tell your husband you think he's special and *why* you're glad you're married to him. Praising your husband will build his self-esteem and make him want to do even better.

Everyone loves to be praised. George Matthew Adams once said, "I don't care how great, how famous, or how successful a man or woman may be, each hungers for applause." Praise is addicting.

Never take for granted that your hubby knows how you feel about him. We aren't the only ones who want to know we're attractive, desirable, and valued. Men want—and need—to feel wanted by their wives. Your husband wants you to want him!

While that goes for all areas of your life and marriage, it especially applies to sex. Your husband wants to know you find him attractive. Sexy. Handsome. Strong. He wants to know that you desire his body, that he turns you on.

Do your best to become your husband's biggest fan. And don't be a fair-weather fan either. One who gives up and stops cheering when her team goes on a losing streak or even has one bad game.

When it comes to cheering for your husband, be like one of those obnoxious guys with the face paint and the wig, the loud voice and pom-poms, the bare chest painted in a rainbow of brilliant colors—even when it's below zero in the middle of a hailstorm.

Cheer on your hubby when he's on a roll—and when he's not doing so hot. Men flock to those who avidly cheer them on. Let your cheers ring the loudest of all.

A Little Experiment

People have a tendency to become what we *encourage* them to be, not what we *nag* them to be. Or said another way—husbands have a tendency to become *what we tell them they are.*

If you tell your husband he is no good, worthless, lazy, forgetful, and immature (and you can do this without words—with eye rolls and loud sighs), he will fulfill your predictions faster than you can blink.

If, on the other hand, you tell him he is thoughtful, wonderful, sensitive, strong, handsome, and brilliant, he will strive to be all that and more. It may not happen overnight, but it will happen.

Don't even try to tell me it's too good to be true. It's not. If you don't believe me, put it to the test. Try it for a month. For one whole month, think of ways every single day that you can affirm, encourage, honor, respect, and build up your husband. And do them! If he has not become more like the man you want him to be in 30 days (not perfect, but a definite improvement), you can bring this book back, and I'll refund your money!

I can imagine the skepticism etched across your face, and you may be thinking one of three things: (1) He won't believe me. (2) He has nothing to compliment. (3) If I let him think he's doing a good job, he'll just keep on doing what he's doing, and he'll never change.

If you are sincere and praise him whenever he comes close to deserving it (it may be hard to come up with things at first!), he *will* believe you because you're telling the truth. And everyone has good qualities—even your husband. You wouldn't have married him if he didn't.

Number three is the excuse I believed for the longest time. "If I compliment him now, he'll think this is good enough, and it will never get any better."

My dear friend, let me tell you something. That seems logical. And it may be. But when it comes to husbands, logic often gets launched out the window.

"Our souls as men yearn for this precious gift [respect] from our wives," Dale Burke says. "It means everything to us. Without it, we will shrivel up and never become the men our wives want us to be. With it, wives, we will take extra pains to care for you the way you long to be cared for."[4]

Go ahead. Try my experiment. You just might like the results. And you may notice some changes in yourself as well. *Gasp!*

In the words of Johann Wolfgang von Goethe—"If you treat a man as he is, he will stay as he is. But if you treat him as if he were what he ought to be and could be, he will become the bigger and better man."

Part Four

Cultivating Family Relationships

7

Family Matters

*Live in harmony with one another...If it is possible,
as far as it depends on you, live at peace with everyone.*

ROMANS 12:16,18

"When you marry your husband, you marry his family." A friend of mine heard these words before she got married and laughed. And then ignored them.

Six months later, she was no longer laughing. She and her husband were having problems. Their relationship with their in-laws was putting a real strain on their marriage.

At one time, most of what Gabe said about my parents was negative—or at least I took it that way. And nearly every comment he made drove me to tears. If I praised my own parents, he took it as a slam on his. I did the same thing and pointed out his parents' faults in rapid succession.

Our parents got along quite well with each other in spite of us, but they *are* very different. In many cases, my parents' weaknesses are Gabe's parents' strengths and vice versa. We were both insecure about our own families, so we resorted to bashing each other's.

In the quest to get along with your in-laws, insecurity is the biggest roadblock. Maybe you're afraid that by accepting his family, you're admitting that the way your family did things is inferior or somehow lacking. A secure person says, "Your way is valid too."

Over time, Gabe and I have grown up considerably. Ask our parents, and they'll nod emphatically and smile widely. For the most part, we have gotten beyond putting down each other's families, but we still have to work at times to understand the idiosyncrasies of our in-laws. Gabe probably more than me.

High Food Pressure

Gabe used to insist that my family had "high food pressure"—a term he concocted for those who get excited at the mere mention of food. Some people have high *blood* pressure. We had high *food* pressure. My sisters and I in particular.

Of course, we've matured over the years, but our excitement about food was sometimes a bit extreme. When a piping hot pizza arrived at our door, we squealed in delight and clapped our hands vigorously. When Mom brought home Soft Batch cookies from the grocery, we jumped up and down. While sitting in the Taco Bell drive-thru, our palms would sweat with anticipation. It's not something to be proud of, but we rarely made attempts to stifle it.

One spring evening, months after our wedding, we were sitting in my parents' living room, not even thinking of food, and someone made mention of one of the many kittens we had when we were growing up. They had all died off—some in a very cruel but accidental manner.

This particular one was named Cocoa Puff. He had eaten fly poison in the barn and met an untimely demise.

"My goodness," Gabe said, "you even named your *cats* after food. Talk about high food pressure."

"We didn't name *all* our cats after food," I protested.

"What were some of their names?" he wanted to know.

"Well, uh…"

"M&M," one of my sisters said.

"Thanks a lot, Bethany. But we're trying to prove Gabe *wrong*."

"Chocolate Chip," my other sister said.

"Stephanie!" My icy glare could have killed her.

"And what about Skittles?" Bethany fondly recalled.

Gabe smirked. "And remember your last dog?" he asked. "His name was Fudge."

"We had a dog named Butterscotch too," Stephanie pointed out.

"I give up!" I said. "I plead guilty to high food pressure!"

Later on that night, I thought of Snuggles, Smidgen, and Joy-Joy, but it was too late to save my reputation.

Batter Up!

Gabe had to get used to the family get-togethers as well. I had grown accustomed to odd behavior in my extended family—my dad's family in particular. But I can only imagine how many times Gabe must have asked himself, "What in the world have I gotten myself into?"

You get any combination of Dad's five opinionated brothers together—and add his sister, Jeannie, to the mix—and you're asking for it. Every last one of them loves to talk. All at once. Loudly.

When we kids could get them to quiet down for just a moment, we did our best to convince them it was time for a rousing game of softball. Nothing compared to the annual family softball game at Grandma and Grandpa's farm. Young and old, small and tall, petite and plump—no one was excluded from the Big Game.

Half the fun was trying to remember all the special rules from years past. Gabe was a bit overwhelmed his first time, but the rules changed so often he wasn't really out of the loop.

Little people got unlimited strikes and sometimes a free trip to first base. Hit the ball over the fence—home run. (Except for the fence west of the barn—that was a ground rule double.) Hit the ball into the branches of the huge oak tree—also a double. Hit a cow in the barnyard—no penalty except for Grandpa's scowl. Hit the shed on the fly—automatic out. Hit the house—*two* automatic outs. Break a window—game over. You know, all your basic softball rules.

You wanted certain people as teammates, and you tried to rig the choosing so you wouldn't be stuck on the losing team. Mothers were pitted against daughters, sons against fathers, brothers against sisters.

Our Big Game slogan came straight from Scripture. "From now on there will be five in one family divided against each other, three against two and two against three. They will be divided, father against son...mother against daughter...mother-in-law against daughter-in-law" (Luke 12:52-53).

We never had enough gloves to go around. The gloveless ones stood in the outfield and watched or retrieved home-run balls. Our bases were old squares of carpet Grandpa kept in the shed. We all perfected our swings and batting stances in order to avoid hitting the buildings along the third base line.

Without fail, someone disagreed with the rules. The arguments were the same year after year, with the same parties involved. For the cousins, those squabbles added spice to the game.

Grandpa would sit on the porch with any of the womenfolk who chose not to play, just waiting for another window to be smashed. We propped up old doors and plywood to cover any panes of glass in harm's way. Grandpa was the unofficial official of the Big Game. No "Play ball!" until all his windows were safe. Sometimes the safety measures took longer than the game itself.

Gabe didn't take long to step right up and become a member of the family. His first at-bat was a colossal home run.

How Are Your Families Different?

Thankfully, although Gabe and I come from different backgrounds, blending into his extended family was painless—and even fun—for me. Two things stand out to me when I think of his kin—their warmth and physical affection, and their joking, teasing nature.

Gabe comes from a long line of huggers and kissers (even though he's not big on PDA himself). When I enter or leave a family gathering, if I don't get a huge hug and a nice big peck on the cheek from each of Gabe's aunts, something's wrong. His dad's side of the family is Italian, so there's a good explanation for all the smooching.

And the teasing and joking! You just can't trust some of Gabe's family—his uncles in particular.

Take Uncle Jim, for instance—a round, jolly guy, not unlike Santa (minus the facial hair). Nice as can be, but completely untrustworthy. If he can pull the wool over your eyes, he's gonna do it.

When I first started dating Gabe, I fell for everything he told me—hook, line, and sinker. These days I don't believe a word he says without concrete evidence and three or more reliable witnesses.

Gabe's dad's brothers often refer to each other (and the rest of us too) in less-than-kind terms—their way of showing affection in a manly way. It's not uncommon to hear one of them call out, "Hey, Ugly!" You hate to even turn around for fear they're actually talking to you (which they usually are).

But the holidays are sure fun with all the hugging and joking and teasing. I rather enjoy the opportunity to brush up on my sarcasm—and my smooching.

How has your husband adjusted to your family? How do you fit in with his? Have the transitions been smooth ones? What strange family traditions have you had to adjust to? Are your families more different than alike?

My family and Gabe's—how are they different? Let me count the ways. We were in the car a few days ago, and I pulled out my little notebook and asked him for some input. I was half afraid to stir things up. Even after six years, discussions about family must be handled with care.

As we talked through some answers, I could sense him treading cautiously as well. It was a beautiful summer evening. Neither of us wanted to spoil it by saying the wrong thing about each other's relations. Here are some things he came up with:

My family uses good grammar, while his family's is less refined, but the way my family corrects each other is somewhat annoying.

Gabe's family likes to talk about the weather, sports, and the goings-on in their community. My family talks about everything under the sun and hasn't learned to talk in turn.

My mom gets really close to people when she talks to them. His mom likes her space. "Everyone a friend!" is my dad's motto. Gabe's dad keeps more to himself.

I'm sure the list could have gone on and on, but we arrived at our destination just in time—while we were still speaking to each other.

I asked women to share the biggest differences between their husbands' families and their own. Then I asked them to go a step further and share how they deal with those differences in a constructive way. If you find one you identify with, perhaps her solution will work for you as well.

> "My family is less involved in our lives, and his family likes to be involved. I have learned that they just want to spend time with us and they are not trying to be nosy."

> "His father was the controller, whereas my mother was. We've had many heated discussions and heartache through the years. We finally stopped trying to change them."

"Everyone in my husband's family has a bad temper and handles conflict poorly. I began praying over every detail and slowly learning how God wanted me to react."

Many newlyweds are shocked that getting used to, or along with, their husbands' families isn't always easy. God created families differently. Getting along with people who are like you in every way is easy. The challenge is building relationships with people who are different from you.

"My husband's family communicates everything with one another. My family hides all negative issues and emotions! My husband and I try to talk about them and compromise."

"My husband has never seen his parents fight. My parents had full-blown (throw things across the room at each other) fights—every day. It's still a struggle for me not to act like my parents. My husband has realized that it's okay to voice his opinion at times."

"My family all are followers of Christ. My husband's brothers are not. They rebelled against God, and their lifestyles are very different from ours. It makes it harder to connect with them, but we really want to see them turn back to God."

No family is perfect—just human. The challenge is to love people, imperfections and all, and to realize that you aren't perfect either. The key is to learn how to deal with your families in a way that brings you and your husband closer together instead of driving you apart.

My sister-in-law Angie commented, "Our families are completely opposite in almost everything. We just accept it and move on—and realize through all their differences they're both great families!"

She's right. Her family and Tug's are as different as they come. But

Tug and Angie are both very open and accepting people, and this has made all the difference.

The Little Things

Sometimes it's the little issues that trip us up—silly things that hardly seem like argument material. Things we've always done without considering that other people (namely our husbands) might do them differently.

Before you were married, you probably hadn't given much thought to how you celebrated holidays. Or what meals were like in your home. What your morning routine looked like or how you spent Sunday afternoons.

How did your family communicate with each other? What was their philosophy about money? Who put gas in the car? Who wrote the checks? How did you open presents, put toilet paper on the roll, and eat your meals?

The family you came from did much to shape the person you are today. You are the product of thousands of little (and big) details, traditions, habits, routines, beliefs, values, and circumstances.

Bathroom Habits

We've all heard newly married women lament the fact that they rarely enter the bathroom and find the toilet seat in its proper location—down. Is that really too much to expect from your new husband?

A male friend of ours once commented on the unfairness of that expectation. "There are two people in the house, right? Let's assume they each use the toilet the same amount of times each day. Why should *I* be the one to move the seat to the position I need it to be in and then move it back for her? I have a better idea. I'll put it down for her when I'm done, and she can put it up for me when she's done!" I have to admit that does sound fair.

What about that darn toilet paper roll? Over? Under? Sitting on the edge of the sink?

"His mom puts the toilet paper on the roll so the sheets unroll from underneath," one of my friends moaned. "Why would anyone do that? It's 'over' all the way!"

So, what if you and your spouse do the toilet paper thing differently? What was your reaction the first time you realized he did it the wrong way? When it comes to these "sensitive" issues, you've got a choice to make. Will you change, try to force *him* to change, or find some sort of compromise?

A friend of mine got her way by default. "We grew up putting the toilet paper roll on differently," she says, "but my way won out because he's too lazy to change the roll!"

What about toothpaste? I don't think Gabe and I have ever argued over it, but my friend April and her husband have. "I never knew squeezing the toothpaste tube from the middle was a sin," she says, "but apparently it is!"

What do you do with your damp towels and washcloths after you use them? Reuse them? Hang them up? Leave them in a pile? Put them in the laundry basket? My friend Jennifer asks her husband to kindly hang his towels up until they dry. For months, she couldn't figure out why their clothes smelled funny even after she'd washed them. She soon realized that Andy was putting wet towels on top of the clothes in the hamper. If she didn't get to the laundry for a while, they started to mildew.

Eating Habits

When, where, and how you eat can cause tension in a marriage if the two of you don't see eye to eye. Did you eat out a lot while growing up, or did your mom have home-cooked meals waiting for you each evening? Did your dad ever cook, or was that strictly Mom's domain? Did you eat around the table, in front of the television, or on the go? Paper plates, good china, or a happy medium?

In days gone by, most moms stayed home and cooked for their families. Everyone sat around the table and talked about their respective days over a hearty meal. That's what I remember growing up, at least until we got to high school and were running all over creation at dinner time.

These days we do try to eat at the table occasionally, but I'm afraid we eat in front of the TV just as often.

One of my friends told me that her husband's family eats dinner in front of the TV and hers has always sat around the kitchen table. "It's just not family time if we're not together around the table," she says.

After a long, tiring day, you might be tempted to collapse in the recliner and let the TV do the talking for you. If you haven't yet adopted this bad habit, don't start now! Try to eat together at the table at least a couple times a week. If your husband is strongly against it, don't nag or argue. Pray about it if it's important to you.

"My family eats out at least once a day," one woman told me, "and my mom never cooks. My husband's family never eats out—his mom cooks every day."

So how do they handle those differences in their marriage? "I don't cook," she says. "If he wants a home-cooked meal, we go to his mom's. She doesn't like that I don't cook, but she'll just have to get over it."

What role did your dad play in the eating game? "My dad didn't think twice about doing the dishes or cooking a meal," one friend told me proudly. "My husband's father doesn't even know how to turn the stove on." It came as a shock when her husband expected her to do all the work in the kitchen.

"My family drinks out of glasses," one friend told me. "His always used Tupperware. He thinks glass tastes funny. How dumb is that?"

Not that dumb, actually. I like plastic better too. Gabe's family uses glasses, but we didn't even have any when I was growing up. Since I'm usually the one pouring the drinks, Gabe and I use plastic 98 percent of the time.

"My family always drank milk straight from the carton," one woman said. "Apparently, that's 'unsanitary, inconsiderate, and gross.'"

I laughed at that one because both our families did the same thing. It bothers me now. I don't mind drinking out of the same container as Gabe, but I think it's gross when any of our family members do it when we're at their house.

Food, Glorious Food!

Going into marriage, I really had no idea that people prepared food in so many different ways. I just assumed that chili was chili, tacos were tacos, and spaghetti was spaghetti. I was shocked the first time I tasted Gabe's mom's cooking. It wasn't better or worse than my mom's—just different.

Gabe's mom uses margarine. My mom likes butter. Gabe's mom makes "dip" eggs for breakfast with buttered bread. My mom makes cheesy scrambled eggs with toast. My mom makes spaghetti by pouring Ragu sauce over long spaghetti noodles. Gabe's mom adds hamburger, olives, onions, and mushrooms and mixes it in with rotini pasta.

I had eaten only traditional lasagna—noodles, sauce, cheese. Gabe's mom loads up her lasagna with eggs, peppers, mushrooms, onions, cheese, noodles, sausage—the kitchen sink. It's surprisingly delicious—one of my favorite meals!

When Gabe's mom makes mashed potatoes, she leaves the skin on and adds onions. My mom peels her potatoes and sometimes adds cheese. My mom and dad drink coffee. Gabe's parents don't. (And Gabe thinks it smells like dirt—go figure.)

Bob Orben once said, "Adam and Eve had an ideal marriage. He didn't have to hear about all the men she could have married, and she didn't have to hear about the way his mother cooked."

I'd imagine most newly married women have heard at least once the dreaded words, "That's not how my mom makes it."

Two months into her marriage, my friend Joy is finding out just how much fun it is to be compared to hubby's dear ol' mom.

The other day, she set out on her weekly trip to the local grocery. One of the items on her list was turkey from the deli. She had been careful to note that her mother-in-law always bought *sliced* turkey, not *chipped* turkey, like Joy had eaten growing up. She knew her husband would like it the way his mom got it and was proud of herself for picking up on this little fact.

She confidently approached the deli. "I'd like a pound of turkey. *Sliced,* please."

"You want that medium or thin?"

It was a simple question for which Joy had no answer. "Uh…oh dear." Maybe she hadn't been as observant as she thought. "Uh, which is most popular?"

"Medium."

Quickly reasoning that it would be best to go with the general consensus and that thin was probably more like chipped anyway, she said, "I'll take medium, please."

The next day, she got out turkey, cheese, and bread and made hubby a sandwich. He took one bite and said, "Ugh! This turkey is sliced too thick! I'm not eating that!"

"What do you mean, you're not eating it?" Joy spouted back.

"It makes me gag. It repulses me. I'm not eating it. You know what my mom gets!"

"I tried to get it like your mom's! Medium-sliced is the same as thin folded over! You're such a baby!"

I don't generally advise calling your husband a baby because it goes against all I'm trying to convey in this book, but I have to admit that Joy's assessment of her husband seemed right on target to me.

Holidays and Celebrations

Speaking of turkey, when it comes to the holidays, newlyweds are often shocked to find that everyone does them differently. Where will you spend each holiday? What does Thanksgiving look like in your home compared to your husband's? Does your family get together for Easter? Memorial Day? New Year's? What traditions do you each have? What kinds of food do you eat? What's the holiday protocol?

Gifts alone are enough to ignite a "discussion" or two between you and your husband. Do you like to be surprised or make wish lists? Do you like practical gifts or fun ones? How many gifts does each person get? For which holidays do you buy them? Do you draw names or buy something for everyone? How much do you spend?

"My family bought few things, but they were quality," one woman told me. "My husband's family were K-Mart bargain shoppers—lots for little."

"His family spends lots of money on everyone's birthdays," another friend commented. "We just don't do that in my family. Who has that kind of money?"

"My husband's family opens Christmas presents youngest to oldest," one friend told me. "In my family, it's a free-for-all."

What about birthdays? In my family, my siblings and I don't usually buy birthday gifts for each other, and we rarely see each other on our birthdays.

Gabe's family always has a small party for him and his brother, and they always buy each other gifts. His mom even buys the non-birthday boy a "good brother" gift.

I had to laugh at one woman's comments. I could have written them myself. "My mom stopped making us birthday cakes when we were about 12," she said. "My husband's mom still makes him a cake every year, and he's almost 30!"

Where you live in relation to both of your families can also cause tension. What if you live close to one set of parents and not the other? It might take a while to work out how you'll divvy up your time during the holidays.

When I asked women what was hardest for them concerning family matters, one woman said, "Spending large amounts of time with his family."

Another noted, "Being close (in distance) to my in-laws and not seeing my own family very often."

And yet another added, "Trying to balance two sets of parents."

Over the years, we've lived anywhere from one to four hours away from our families. Typically, we alternate spending Christmas morning with each set of parents. This year, we live closer, and we'll spend that special time with our girls in our own home and see our parents later that day.

Joanne Heim shares an interesting Thanksgiving she celebrated with her in-laws. She and Toben lived in Pennsylvania, and his folks lived in Colorado. When Toben's parents visited them for a week in November, they celebrated all the holidays at once.

One day was Easter with an egg hunt and ham for dinner. One day was New Year's with party food. One day was Christmas with gifts for all. One day they celebrated everyone's birthdays with a cake and balloons. And of course, they celebrated Thanksgiving.[1] What a fun week that must have been!

Understanding Why

Sometimes we just don't get why our in-laws do what they do. When your husband or a member of his family says or does something that makes no sense to you, take the opportunity to find out the story behind it. This gesture can go a long way in clearing up a slew of questions or misunderstandings you may have.

The key to dealing with family differences is making an honest effort to understand why your husband's family does what they do. You still may not like their habits, but understanding where your husband is coming from is helpful, and you might learn something.

As a teacher, I quickly learned that any child who consistently misbehaved or disobeyed had some deeper problem. One boy watched his dad beat up his mom nearly every day until she left him. One girl had been sexually abused for most of her young life.

These are extreme examples, but they demonstrate basic cause and effect. We do things for a reason. Everybody has a story, and sometimes a deeper understanding of your husband's story can make all the difference.

Let your husband know you're interested in his family history. "Honey, I really want to get to know your family and understand them better. I'd love any insight you can give me into why they do this or that particular thing."

Ask kind and thoughtful questions about your husband's family each time the opportunity arises. The *way* you ask is key. Make sure your motives are pure. Don't be pushy or nosy, prying into things your husband doesn't want to share.

In addition to learning your husband's story, be open-minded. Try something new—you might like it! My philosophy? When in Rome, do as the Romans do! And with Gabe's Italian family, that motto packs a new punch!

Fight the Urge to Criticize His Family

Here's a nugget of wisdom for you: When an opportunity arises (and it will) to criticize a member of your husband's family—to point out unattractive qualities in his mom, brother, or grandma—hold your tongue!

Here's why. Chances are, those little quirks and annoying traits are every bit as irksome and irritating to him as they are to you—but don't you be the one to tell him! Those negative feelings he has toward that bothersome relative are just going to get transferred over to you—whether he means to do it or not.

You know what it's like. You can criticize your dad till the cows come home, but heaven forbid your husband should criticize him. How dare he voice his negative opinion of your beloved father!

If your husband is frustrated with his mom or sister and feels as if he can't do anything about it—and you open your big mouth—he's going to take his frustration out on you.

Gabe and I have witnessed this phenomenon transpiring before our very eyes one too many times. Somewhere along the line, we both learned to keep quiet about each other's families.

These days, we typically wait until the other one brings up his or her own family and then just listen and nod occasionally. Sometimes we'll cautiously agree with each other, quietly verbalizing our support.

On occasion, we'll even—*gasp!*—defend each other's families. Just yesterday, I found myself saying, "Aw, give your mom a break. You know she's just trying to do what's best for you." Who'd have thought?

If your husband criticizes your family, do your best to keep from getting defensive. He might be saying things just to be spiteful, or he might not. What he's saying could contain some truth, even if you don't want to hear it.

Gabe has done an awesome job of accepting my family in the past couple years. I used to cry myself to sleep sometimes, wondering if they'd ever be compatible, let alone friends.

Now he listens to them, respects them, and does his best never to criticize them. Prayer works! Hallelujah!

Leave and Cleave

You also need to address the failure of one or both of you to leave Mom and Dad and cleave to each other. We'll talk about hubby's mom extensively in the next chapter, but what about you and your own parents? Do you and your husband see eye to eye on the amount of time you spend with your family? Do you run to Mom with every marital problem?

As a wife, your husband comes first. Then your family. God says so. You don't have to forsake your family—the command to love and honor your mom and dad still stands. But your primary loyalty should be to your husband. He should also be your biggest priority in terms of time, love, affection, and communication.

Do your marriage a favor—don't run to Mom every time (or anytime) you and hubby get in a fight. The best thing you can do is go to God first. Moms are not objective about fights between their baby girls and the man who stole them away.

Besides, you want your mom to love your husband. This will be hard for her to do if you're constantly sharing his faults. Unless you're prepared to call and share each and every thing he does *right* in his life, don't call and tell her when he messes up!

Friends of ours had a rough year in their marriage, and they actually separated for a while. She comments that "we let our parents have too much input into our lives and marriage. We decided it was a big problem and put a stop to it."

You may not agree on how much time to spend with your families. Just make sure you communicate openly about how you feel.

My friend Teri shared with me that in the beginning, she was bothered by the amount of time her husband, Wes, spent with his dad in their family business. She finally shared with him how she felt. Wes explained his thoughts on the matter, and they came to an agreement that satisfied them both. By being open and vulnerable, Teri saved herself from potential resentment and bitterness toward Wes.

Talk to your husband if "family time" is a concern of yours, and respect his opinion. If you honestly feel he is being unfair or unreasonable, pray about it. God, the great Arbitrator and Judge, can do far more to change your hubby's heart than you ever could. He may even end up changing your heart instead.

He'll honor your request for your will and your husband's to line up with each other. It may take time—those things always do. While you're waiting, submit to your husband—even if it kills you. (It won't.)

He's Not Your Dad

One woman told me, "I compared my husband to my dad. He is not my dad, and I realized he wasn't raised like my dad was, so I surrendered the hope."

This one's tough. Any woman blessed with a kind, loving father—especially one who was a spiritual leader in her home—has been given an incredible gift. We often fail to realize, though, that the dads we knew and loved were older and more mature than our husbands. Most of us remember our dads best when they were in their thirties and forties, not when they were newlyweds.

Don't forget—we didn't know our dads as husbands either. As children, we only see one side of our fathers. Our dads treated us differently than they did our moms. If you don't want your husband to compare you to his mom, don't compare him to your dad.

On the other hand, many women enter marriage with a terrible idea of men because of their bad experiences with their fathers. One of my friends told me that it was hard to trust her husband at first. "I had built a wall because of things my dad did," she said.

Again, you aren't being fair to your husband when you transfer those negative feelings to him. He's not your dad. He's your husband. Don't fall into the trap of comparing hubby to daddy. It's a no-win situation regardless of how you look at it.

The Merge

"You marry your partner's script of what marriage and family look like," Joanne Heim says.[2] I couldn't agree more. The key is learning to understand each other's scripts, getting past the differences in them, and trying your best to follow along—and staying on the same page!

Eventually, you'll write your own script together as a family, but that will take a while. Your new script will be a combination of the original scripts with your own special additions over the years.

"One of the truly great things about getting married is the chance to adopt another history that weaves together with your own to create a fabric that is similar to the one your parents wove but is also unique to your new family of two."[3]

Have a blast creating your very own quaint and quirky family quilt!

8

Your Hubby, Her Baby

*I've been told all about what you
have done for your mother-in-law…
May you be richly rewarded by the Lord.*

Ruth 2:11-12

Whether they deserve it or not, mothers-in-law get a bad rap. Of all the questions in my survey, the ones about hubby's mama got the most heated response.

"My mother-in-law doesn't know how to butt out," one woman said. "She doesn't understand that her kids are adults and have their own decisions to make." She wasn't the only one who felt that way.

What words come to mind when you think of your mother-in-law? Do they have a positive connotation, or are they mostly negative?

Did any of the following make your list: selfish, rude, nosy, critical, opinionated, overbearing, bossy, or controlling?

If not, then (1) You've been married less than three months, or (2) your mother-in-law lives in another country, and you never see her, or (3) you're in denial. (Just kidding!)

It All Started So Smoothly

I know many women who began dating their now-husbands and developed a nice friendship with their mother-in-law-to-be. Then they got married. And that lovely friendship went out the window.

My friend Jessie comments, "It was pretty good before we got married. We talked. We got along. Afterward, it started going downhill."

Why the big change? Well, here's how I see it. When you're dating a guy, you want his mom to like you, to accept you as part of the family. You want her to be happy that her son has chosen you. Then you get married, and your "want list" changes drastically.

(1) You want to do everything right when it comes to being a wife—whether it's cooking, cleaning, or managing your home and life. (2) You want to be the center of your husband's world.

That's not too much to ask, right? But there's a small problem. There sits your mother-in-law who (1) has 20-plus more years of experience in home and life management than you have and (2) has been the center of your husband's world for his entire existence.

Other factors might add fuel to the fire as well. Maybe hubby is Mama's only boy or the baby of the family. Maybe his mom is a single parent or had a bad relationship with her husband. Maybe her background is different from yours. Maybe the two of you are way too much alike and see each other as competition.

Can any mother- and daughter-in-law possibly have a warm and loving relationship? Of course.

She Didn't Stand a Chance

Gabe's mom, Janelle, and I are a lot alike—assertive, independent, "I'll do that myself, thanks" kind of girls. That worked out fine for Janelle as a mom. Her boys were more than happy to let her take charge—especially if that meant less work for them.

Then along comes Little Miss Independent Daughter-in-Law, who doesn't want anything done for her—or her husband. Janelle had been taking care of Gabe for 21 years, loving and providing for him, and I made it pretty clear once we got married that she could hand in her uniform and pick up her last check.

You take a mother who has done things for her son his entire life and add a new wife who has done things for herself her entire life, and something's gotta give. Janelle's love language was acts of service. She would do things for me and Gabe as an expression of love. I took her help as an insult and an insinuation that I was incapable of doing a good enough job on my own.

I was so inconsistent. I didn't mind when Janelle came to visit and took five loads of laundry to the Laundromat. I hated the place. However, when she changed the sheets on our bed without asking if they needed to be changed (I'd done it the day before), I was hopping mad. Or the time she mopped our kitchen floor, assuming I hadn't done it in a while (again, the day before). She was only trying to help, but she ended up feeling stupid, and I gloated.

I remember Janelle writing me a letter once and thanking me for taking such good care of Gabe, for cooking good meals for him, doing his laundry, keeping our home clean, and the like. After reading those words, I had two options.

I could either think, "Wow—I'm glad she appreciates me. It's not every day I get thanked for fixing dinner and cleaning the house. After I took her job and everything!"

Or I could think something vindictive—"I can't believe her nerve! All she cares about is her little boy and making sure he's spoiled rotten for the rest of his life. I'm not some glorified maid picking up where she left off—doing all the dirty work so her little prince doesn't have to lift a precious finger! Wait till Missy hears about this! She'll *die!*"

I took the low road—then and many other times.

Once, she sent Gabe a box full of new underwear, socks, and shorts, and I fumed. Never mind that she had just saved us tons of money. Gabe wouldn't need new undergarments for months. But I complained that she was still acting like his mommy and wouldn't butt out of his life. "And why wasn't there anything in the box for me?" I demanded to know (even though I'm sure I would have been outraged if my mother-in-law had dared pick out bras and panties for yours truly).

Thanks to me, she really didn't have a snowball's chance in an oven. Try as she might, she just couldn't win.

Apron Strings

I have a friend whose mother-in-law is absolutely convinced that her son can do no wrong. I happen to know from personal experience (I went to college with him) that he has pulled the wool of a few mammoth sheep over mama's eyes. I won't accuse him of lying, but he has certainly never corrected her when she says things like, "My son would never do anything like that." Or "My son has never lied (or sworn or drunk beer)."

It's tough for my friend when her mother-in-law "knows without a doubt" that any problems are her *daughter-in-law's* fault. Her son, after all, is faultless. Thankfully, while Gabe's mom loves him dearly, she isn't holding on to any notions of his perfection.

Along those same lines, some mamas often have a hard time letting go of their little guys. One friend told me, "I see my husband as my husband—a man. She still sees him as her child—a boy."

Another woman complained, "She is way too involved in his life. She doesn't treat him as an adult. It's like she's holding on to the idea that he's still her baby at 22."

Believe it or not, it isn't always mama that can't let go. I find it interesting that God directed His command to leave Mom and Dad and be united to your mate to the *man,* even though it applies both ways. Maybe God geared His speech toward Adam because guys generally have more trouble with this.

My sister Bethany agrees. "The possessive-mother instinct isn't a problem with Stewart's mom," she says. "At this point, Stewart is the one who doesn't want to let go."

Do you find yourself getting irritated and frustrated because your husband won't loosen his grip on those strings that have tied him to Mom for so many years? You are right to want him to leave his parents and cleave to you. But this doesn't mean he has to end his relationship with Mom and Dad. Where do you draw the line?

Take the matter to God in prayer. Then discuss it openly with your husband at a time when you're both calm and in a good mood. Changes may be slow in coming, but nagging and whining will never help.

Ideally, your hubby will be hopelessly devoted to you, his adored leading lady, with Mom playing a much lesser, secondary role. This is not always the case.

Do try to think of it from your husband's perspective. Most moms love their kids unconditionally—it just comes naturally. Wives, on the other hand, must work much harder at loving their husbands without conditions attached.

If your hubby has a mother who went out of her way to treat him like a prince, who would want to give that up? Especially if his new wife doesn't always seem to have his best interests at heart. Loosening those strings would mean doing a lot more for himself. How fun is that?

What Do I Call Her?

Several women told me that one of the hardest things for them was figuring out what to call their mother-in-law.

"It sounds kind of stupid," a friend of mine said, "but I don't know what to call his mom. I don't feel really comfortable calling her mom (yet anyway), but I don't want to insult her by being too formal either."

I have a couple friends who call their mothers-in-law Mom, but Janelle told me right away that "I'll never be Mom to anyone but Gabe and Tug." Initially, I was hurt—and ticked. Now I'm glad we had that talk because I've only called her Janelle, and it's perfectly comfortable for both of us. Calling her Mom would have been awkward.

One woman shared with me that for the first couple of years of her marriage, she didn't know what to call her in-laws, so she didn't call them anything at all. Once she had children, problem solved. Hubby's mom and dad became Grandma and Grandpa to everyone. If you're stumped by the in-law name game, hurry up and have a baby! (I am *so* kidding.)

Insecurity Issues

What is it about a mother-in-law that causes us newly married women to experience so many negative emotions? I have a guess—our own sinful attitudes.

"Wait just a second!" you argue, "*I* am not the problem here. You don't know my mother-in-law!" No, I don't. And I don't know you either. "I am not the problem" is what I would have said seven years ago in my defense against my own mother-in-law. Today, things are different, and I'll explain a little later.

So your mother-in-law has issues, but we're going to start with you and me. Insecurity is the main problem from which many other sinful attitudes stem. I see insecurity manifested in many different ways.

Deep down, we're often afraid that we won't be a good enough wife to our husband, that his mom won't like us, that we won't live up to her expectations.

My friend Pat shared her initial insecurities. "Having Rick's mom pamper him when she came to visit always made me feel like I wasn't a good enough wife," she says.

One woman admitted, "I've always felt that she's not quite sure I can take care of him," while another said, "I didn't know if she thought I was a good mate for her son."

One friend told me she struggled for a while being completely herself around her mother-in-law. She felt like she had to impress her.

One woman was pregnant when she got married and was afraid of what her mother-in-law thought of her.

One friend had a hard time reading her mother-in-law and couldn't tell when she was joking. Another struggled because her mother was an encourager, but her mother-in-law never verbalized her approval.

One woman shared that "I had a little bit of a desire to be treated like a daughter, but I knew that she already had three daughters. Maybe she didn't feel like she needed another one." She put up a wall between them to keep from getting hurt.

I've done the same thing with Janelle. By keeping her at a distance, I kept her from getting too close, from seeing my imperfections. I didn't want to be vulnerable. I wanted to keep my edge. Pride snuck in too, saying, "I don't need a relationship with you. I'm perfectly happy keeping you on the outside looking in."

Insecurity also masquerades as jealousy when we don't want to share our husbands with their mothers or we become resentful of the closeness they might share.

"The hardest thing for me," one friend confided, "was sharing my husband's affections with her. I was jealous."

I want to be the world's best expert on my husband, not play second fiddle to his mother. I don't want him sharing more intimacy with her than with me.

A secure wife will get to know her husband as wholly and completely as she can and willingly share him with others, not worrying that his affection for her will be diminished. A secure wife doesn't have hostile feelings toward others.

Have you considered the fact that your mother-in-law may be insecure too? Or envious of you? Maybe you're prettier than her, or skinnier, or smarter. If nothing else, you're much younger (unless you're a cradle-robber). She may feel as if you've taken her place in her son's life.

Why not step up and tell her, "I don't love *my* mom any less now that I'm married. Neither does your son love you any less."

When we're insecure, we make unhealthy and inaccurate comparisons between ourselves and others. "Don't compare yourself with others," Galatians 6:4 (MSG) says. "Each of you must take responsibility for doing the creative best you can with your own life."

Take time to understand her perspective. Meet in the middle—even if you're the only one moving. When you get along with your mother-in-law, you are giving your husband one of the most precious gifts you can give.

Offer Forgiveness

If the women I surveyed are telling the unjaded truth, a few of the mothers-in-law out there are giving the whole bunch a bad name.

"She was hardheaded and opinionated and never wrong!" one woman said of her mother-in-law. Then she admitted, "I was no angel with her. Until years later…when God grew me more and more. She didn't change, but how I reacted to her changed."

"It was hard reaching out to be Christlike," one friend told me. "I set myself up to be rejected."

"No one is good enough to please her," one woman said. "She is a miserable person who blames others for her misery."

"I was called every name in the book and treated like trash," said another woman. "Over the years, I have learned to be like Jesus regardless of how she acts, and I pray that she'll see how He can change her life if she would just trust!"

We find it hard to forgive people who hurt us, but Jesus forgave the people who were murdering Him—as they did it. He didn't dwell on the hurt for a time, wallow in it a little, feel sorry for Himself, tell His friends about it, and plot revenge of all varieties in His heart (as we might do with our mothers-in-law). No, He showed us a perfect example of complete forgiveness.

"I've tried to forgive her," you say. "I just can't!"

Of course you can't. Forgiveness like that is not in our power. But Christ's power dwells in us. He can forgive *through* you if you ask Him. If you have a rotten mother-in-law, ask God to help you love and forgive her. And if you're the one being rotten, ask Him to forgive you and help you turn your relationship around.

A Bitter Heart

Speaking of rotten daughters-in-law, this week I nearly chucked this entire chapter. "I don't *really* need a mother-in-law chapter in this book, do I?" I asked myself bitterly as I dangled my hard copy over the trash can.

God was throwing a test my way—as He has done countless times during the writing of this book. "So you want to write about marriage, do you?" He said with a smile. "The words just flow from your pen, don't they? Let's see how you do when you're confronted with some of these same issues in your own marriage."

Some of the tests I've been given in the last year include making time for Gabe when I have "more important" things to do, deciding to enjoy sex when I wasn't in the mood, loving my sisters-in-law without envy or jealousy, submitting to my husband when I think he's wrong, accepting Gabe's family, canceling the self-pity galas, not being a critical nag, keeping my mouth shut, and trusting God to convict my husband.

Some of the tests I've passed, and others I have failed.

This week has been an intense spiritual battle over the subject of this chapter—my mother-in-law. I'd love to share the details—color them to favor my side, of course—and continue to bask in my horrid attitude.

Instead, I've finally taken the step of saying, "Lord, take away my bitterness. Take my focus off myself and place it on You, where it belongs. Help me give this completely over to You. Bitterness is sin, and it's eating away at me. Spirit, work in my heart, and scrape every last bit of resentment from its walls. You and bitterness can't coexist in my heart, and I need *You* to stay. Show me where I've sinned, and please forgive me."

I felt so free after praying that prayer, yet the battle against envy and resentment isn't over—and I can't win it on my own. My relationship with Gabe's mom improves with each passing year, but Satan still likes to attack it every now and again.

The Model Daughter-in-Law

Picture your mother-in-law in your mind. Now pretend her husband (your father-in-law) has just died. You are married to one of her two sons—the better-looking one of course! You, your husband, your brother-in-law, sister-in-law, and mother-in-law enjoy ten years together as a family.

Then your husband and his brother both die suddenly. You have no children, nor does your sister-in-law. You three women are left with no ties among you now that the men in your lives are gone.

Your mother-in-law plans to return to her native land. You and your sister-in-law make plans to go with her. She won't hear of it. "Go back to your families," she tells you. "I have nothing to offer you.

Even if I remarried and had more sons, you'd be old women by the time they grew up!"

Your sister-in-law weeps, kisses her husband's mother for the last time, and tearfully goes back to her family to grieve. But you cling to your mother-in-law and say, "Don't urge me to leave you or to turn back from you. Where you go I will go, and where you stay I will stay. Your people will be my people and your God my God." You go with her, leaving behind the only home you've ever known.

On some level, your mother-in-law must appreciate your sacrifice, but outwardly, there aren't many signs. "The Almighty has made my life very bitter," she cries. "I went away full, but the Lord has brought me back empty."

She doesn't welcome you with open arms or take comfort in your fellowship and the love you both shared for her son. She doesn't seem to acknowledge that you have significant worth as your own person. Even still, you stay by her side.

Your loyalty runs so deep that only a short time after you bury your beloved husband, you marry an older man you barely know so your mother-in-law's family name can be carried on. Even then, her neighbors have to remind her of your value. You are worth more to her than seven sons, they say.

Because of your loyalty and faithfulness to a woman you call mother-in-law, God allows you to become the great-grandmother of your country's greatest king and an ancestress of the King of Kings.

In case you didn't recognize this story, it comes from the Old Testament book of Ruth. Ruth could have been bitter against the God of Israel for taking her husband, but she wasn't. Her devotion was deep despite her mother-in-law Naomi's bitterness and callousness. Now *that* is unconditional love. What a timeless example Ruth is to daughters-in-law everywhere.

My Sister by Marriage

We'll wrap up our discussion on mothers-in-law in a moment, but Ruth's story got me thinking about another female in-law. Ruth's sister-in-law, Orpah, makes just a brief appearance in chapter 1, but I can't help but wonder what their relationship was like while their husbands were still living. Were they best friends who confided in each other and got along famously? Or were they more like rivals, constantly competing against each other? I wish we knew.

The sister-in-law relationship can be a complicated one. My two sisters-in-law and I have worked through a number of situations where we have envied or resented each other. I'm thankful that both of them have made a conscious effort to maintain a good, sisterly relationship with me—even when it wasn't easy.

Your Hubby's Sis

"I'm glad you don't have any sisters," I said to Gabe the other day as we sat in the bleachers at a college football game. I nodded my head toward the threesome sitting in front of us—a young man sandwiched between his sister and his girlfriend.

Mr. Macho would spend a few moments cuddling up to his girlfriend, giving her a peck, squeezing her waist, whispering in her ear. Then the next minute, he'd turn toward his sister, laugh, and talk, their faces close together.

Girlfriend would scowl if he lingered too long with Little Sis. She'd move his arm around her own waist and turn his face toward hers for a kiss. He'd spend a few more moments with Girlfriend and then turn his attention back toward his sibling.

I couldn't help but think how I would have dealt with Gabe having sisters. Would I have been the jealous girlfriend? I asked my brother's wife, Jessica, for some input. She married a man with three sisters.

"When I first married Josh, I wanted to be like a sister," Jess told me, "but knew you each already had two perfectly good sisters. Maybe you didn't need another one. At first, I just sat and watched because I didn't want anyone to think I was trying to butt in. I felt like an outsider. I soon realized that becoming a 'sister' would take effort."

"I'm sure you guys felt the same way," she continued. "'How are we supposed to treat her? Does she want to get involved?' At the same time, I was thinking, 'How am I supposed to act? Do they want to include me?'"

Instead of feeling sorry for herself, Jess looked at her circumstances from Josh's sisters' perspective, not just her own. A good example to follow.

One friend told me that she can't talk about certain things around her husband's sister. "It's hard to open up to her because my husband is her brother. I don't think we'll ever be close friends. It's uncomfortable when she criticizes my husband. I know she's just acting like an older sister, but when she tells my husband he's annoying, how am I supposed to respond?"

What would *you* do? Defend hubby? Or keep things running smoothly with his sis?

My inexperienced advice would be to pray about it first. Then talk to your husband to get his opinion. Maybe he hasn't even noticed the conflict. Then one of you could talk to his sister about how her comments affect you.

The important thing is to be determined to work at the relationship. You don't have to be best friends, but there shouldn't be ill feelings between you.

My sister Bethany just got married this past summer. Stewart, her husband, is one of six children and has two sisters. Bethany thinks that having sisters has helped Stewart understand girls better than a lot of guys do.

I know a guy whose wife isn't so fortunate. Blake has three brothers and no sisters and a lot to learn about women. He gets irritated when his wife and her mom and sister talk about things like PMS.

"My mom *never* complained about that stuff," he once told me. "She was *tough*. Growing up, we never even knew when she was on her period." (As if Mom was going to get all chatty with her four boys about tampons and menstrual cramps. C'mon, Blake.)

Married to Brothers

The sister-in-law you might have the most in common with is your brother-in-law's wife, even though you're the most distantly related. You married brothers, you have the same mother-in-law, and your own families are safely out of the picture. Bethany has gained insight by talking to the women who married Stewart's brothers. "I understand now why Stewart does some of the things he does," she says. "The brothers are all the same! I realized it wasn't just Stewart's problem but a family thing. It helps make some of his quirks seem more funny than annoying."

That's the good part. Then there's the other side of the equation—the competition and rivalry that often exists between two women who married brothers. I have a friend who constantly struggles with feeling inferior to her brother-in-law's wife.

"She's so perfect," my friend says. "Tall, thin, beautiful, talented—I could never measure up to her. My husband's parents have nothing but praise for her. They have plenty of negative things to say about me."

I remember when Angie married Gabe's brother, Tug. I couldn't help feeling envious of her—young, petite, and gorgeous. I compared myself to her time after time and wasn't happy unless I came out on top, which wasn't that often. I even rejoiced when she struggled with areas that came easily to me.

Then one day, Angie called me on the phone and told me she had to get something off her chest. Through tears, she shared that she had been jealous of me for various reasons and had even said some negative things about me to others.

How did that make me feel? Honestly, I felt a huge weight being lifted. So, it wasn't just me! We were envious of each other for the dumbest reasons. I was jealous of her petite, curvy figure. She was jealous of my height. I was jealous because I thought she was prettier than me. She was jealous because she thought I was smarter than her. We forgave each other and our relationship took a 180-degree turn.

Why do we always have to be better than someone else to be happy? I have to be smarter or prettier or better dressed or a better writer or have more money or a better marriage. If I'm not or I don't, I'm jealous, bitter, envious, discontented—pick a word, any word.

Focusing on Christ—not me—is the key to overcoming this selfish, sinful attitude. When I read God's Word, spend time in prayer, reach out to others, and take the focus off myself, this becomes less of a struggle.

I simply love 1 Corinthians 4:7 (MSG): "Isn't everything you *have* and everything you *are* sheer gifts from God? So what's the point of all this comparing and competing?" I'm glad Angie and I figured that out when we did.

Her Mother-in-Law, Your Mom

One of the most challenging aspects of your relationship with your brother's wife is that her mother-in-law is your dear mom. You know how it is. It's okay for you to criticize your own family, but heaven forbid someone else dare criticize them, especially someone who married into the family.

I used to feel that way about Jessica until I took the plank out of my eye. I could say negative things about *my* husband's mom and not think anything of it, but if Jessica said negative things about *her* husband's mom, it was personal, and I took offense.

Pointing out Jessica's unfairness to her mother-in-law was easy for me because I was being unfair to my own. I had a three-year head start on Jessica in the getting-along-with-your-mom-in-law depart-ment, and sometimes you couldn't even tell.

So what is my advice for getting along with your brother's wife? Put yourself in her shoes, especially when it comes to your mom. If I wanted people to love me despite my struggles with Janelle, wasn't it only fair to love Jessica despite any struggles she might have with her mother-in-law?

On a similar note, maybe you don't like how your sister-in-law treats her husband (your brother). My suggestion is to pray for her, for her marriage, and for God to help you love her regardless of her actions. Remember—you don't know what it's like to be married to your brother. You may love him dearly as a sibling, but being his wife is quite another story.

On Friendly Terms

It's only fair that I include some happy thoughts about our hus-bands' moms. I was pleased to find that many women get along really well with their mothers-in-law. Here's what some of them had to share.

> "I don't think my mother-in-law has one enemy. She is always serving others."

> "I respect her and admire her instincts as a mother! She raised a wonderful son!"

> "She has always been very accepting of me."

> "She respects me as a person and recognizes my wife position."

"She is not a critical person, and I get along with those types of people best."

"She has never interfered with our family relationships or decisions."

"She sees me as a positive influence on my husband."

"She is the most loving, accepting person I have ever met."

"I think she knows I truly love her son and want him to succeed."

Others have to work harder at friendship but find that the effort really pays off. Hopefully, we can learn something from them.

"I made a decision to make it work. I pray for us."

"I am honest with her. We take time to talk and be together."

"I try to give her time with her son when we visit."

"I let her know how I feel, but I've also learned when to keep my thoughts to myself. I don't always have to be right. I know she treasures him."

"I always try to respect her and honor her. It is a give-and-take relationship."

Her Side of the Story

Any negative attitudes I have toward Janelle often quickly change when I put on her shoes and start walking. She has told me that she knows she's not very good at the mother-in-law thing. For 21 years she was a loving, doting, self-sacrificing mother. With one little wedding, all that changed. Not only did she have to rethink her role as a mother and let go of so much she had invested in the past 21 years, she also had a new member of her family to worry about—someone related to her in a strange new way.

Being a mom came naturally to her—she loved her baby boy with all of her heart from the very beginning. And she had years and years to practice being a good mom.

Being a mother-in-law is a different story. You get no time to practice. You're just thrust into this foreign role and expected (by your daughter-in-law and others) to get it right. You go from being a boy's mom to being the mother of a man and mother-in-law to his new wife.

Some women may adjust better than others to this new role, but I'm not sure any mother makes the transition with 100 percent ease. If I ever have a son, I will better understand what it's like to lose him to another woman.

It also helps to know your mother-in-law's story. In Janelle's case, there are very good reasons why she acted in certain ways early in my marriage to Gabe. Knowing and appreciating her story made a huge difference. Discovering why your mother-in-law acts the way she does is a key to opening the doors of friendship.

When I asked Janelle to share with me a struggle she had with her own mother-in-law, she said, "She had a tough life. I needed to respect that more. I was too young to realize all that she went through." I could say the same thing about Janelle.

I need to believe the best about people. That includes giving Janelle the benefit of the doubt when she says something that I could take either as an offensive statement or a harmless one. Most of our struggles have been due to sinful attitudes on my part. With time and prayer, things have gotten steadily better, and I thank God for her.

In recent months, Janelle has made a concerted effort to reach out to me, break down walls I'd built around myself, praise me for various things, and get to know me better in many ways. She loves our daughters like they are her own, and I know she would lay down her life not just for them or Gabe but for me as well.

We laugh and cry together and feel comfortable sharing deep heart issues with each other. God has used her in a mighty way to soften my heart, and I love her more than I have at any other point. At this stage of the game, I am happy and thankful to call Janelle my friend.

If you're not at this point yet, don't despair. You can do it too—with a big helping of God's love and grace.

Learning to Love

Because loving others is a command in the Bible, God promises to give us the strength we need to obey that command. Remember back in chapter 3 when we talked about loving our husbands like Paul describes in 1 Corinthians 13? Love is patient, kind, and all that?

Well, it was one thing to apply those love qualities to our husbands, the ones we handpicked to spend the remainder of our days with, but what about my husband's *mother?* Do I love *her?* I mean, really, really love her, as in the 1 Corinthians kind of love?

Let's see how we fare on the "mother-in-law love test."

Love is patient. That means giving my mother-in-law time to adjust to her new role. Patience means not expecting perfection from her immediately but allowing her time to learn and grow. Being patient includes giving her a break when she forgets that her baby boy is all grown up now and belongs to me.

Love is kind. This means speaking only words that build up my mother-in-law, not tear her down. Kindness should show up in my actions as well. Kindness is sending my mother-in-law a "just because I care" card, thanking her for raising her son to be such a wonderful husband.

It does not envy. Love does not envy when my husband calls his mother on the phone to chat, or says, "I wonder what advice my mom would give me about this." Love does not envy when my mother-in-law brings up all the fun their family used to have together before I came on the scene. Love does not envy when my husband's mom buys him the perfect birthday present—and he likes it better than mine.

It does not boast. Love never says, "I told you so!" Not even when I am proven right and my mother-in-law is proven wrong. Love doesn't brag about my talents, accomplishments, or anything else.

It is not proud. Love is not too proud to admit I'm wrong or have made a mistake. Love is not too proud to ask my mother-in-law for forgiveness when I hurt her feelings. Love is not too proud to say, "I don't know the solution to this problem. You have more experience in this area. Could you help me?"

It is not rude. Love isn't sarcastic, biting, scathing, or cruel. It doesn't roll its eyes or make nasty comments to my mother-in-law's face or behind her back.

It is not self-seeking. Love doesn't hog my husband but shares him with his mother (and father, sisters, and brothers).

It is not easily angered. Love's first response to my mother-in-law's seemingly insensitive comments is not to get angry but to try to see things from her point of view, even giving her the benefit of the doubt.

It keeps no record of wrongs. Love doesn't bring up my mother-in-law's past offenses every time I get irritated with her. Love doesn't keep a list (mental or otherwise) of everything she has ever done wrong, every sin (real or imagined) she's ever committed.

Love does not delight in evil. Love doesn't derive secret pleasure out of my mother-in-law's sins and shortcomings because I think they make me look better.

But rejoices with the truth. Love means being truthful to my mother-in-law even when I don't want to own up to something I've done.

It always protects. Love protects my mother-in-law's reputation and her feelings. This can only happen if I never say a bad word about her. When she makes a big mistake, if it's no big deal, I let it slide.

Always trusts. Love takes my mother-in-law at her word. If she says she loves and appreciates me, I believe her.

Always hopes. Love believes that with prayer, things can get better between my mother-in-law and me. It doesn't throw its hands up and say, "This is a lost cause!" Love means having an optimistic outlook on the future of our relationship.

Always perseveres. Love never gives up on my relationship with my mother-in-law, even if it seems irreparable. Love doesn't shrug and say, "Forget it! Who needs her?" Love keeps going, even when the only thing I want to do is quit.

Love never fails. Love says, "God will love me forever, regardless of what I do. I'll love my mother-in-law forever too."

Take some time today to pray for your mother-in-law. Whether you feel like it or not, ask God to help you learn to love her with a 1 Corinthians kind of love. Remember—He promises to give you what you need to do just that.

Part Five

Fanning
the Flames

9

The Marriage Bed

A man will leave his father and mother and
be united to his wife, and they will become one flesh.

GENESIS 2:24

So tell me, did you open this book and skip right to this chapter? Come on. Be honest. I do the same thing! If it's about sex, I want to read it!

At first, I hesitated to include a chapter on sex in this book. Sharing personal details on the topic can be uncomfortable—especially for my husband! But I know that sex is a very important part of marriage, and I'm sure *I'd* be disappointed in any marriage book that didn't include a chapter (or two or six) on the subject. I've tried to be as candid as I could without invading the privacy of our marriage bed. (Ha! This entire book violates our privacy!)

Sex is a private thing between you and your husband—truly the only thing you share with him alone. Sure, there is a time to share with others—usually to encourage a sister in Christ in her marriage (as this book will hopefully do). But in today's society, people discuss their sex lives with the world like they're talking about the weather.

Your sexual relationship with your husband deserves privacy and respect. Don't share juicy details with your girlfriends like teenage boys in a locker room. Intimacy isn't intimacy when shared with others.

You're Unique (Sort Of)

I wish I knew you personally. I wish we could sit down and have a chat about our lives and marriages. I wish I could address your specific concerns about sex. Maybe you're newly married, you saved yourself for marriage, and you're enjoying sex immensely. Or you might have saved yourself for marriage, but you're miserable in bed. Maybe sex hurts—every single time.

Perhaps you've been married three years and never had an orgasm. Maybe you want sex more than your husband does. Maybe you were sexually abused as a child or even as an adult. Perhaps you can't seem to pick up the pieces of your sexual past. You might feel depressed after every lovemaking experience and have no idea why. You could be at any point on the married-sex spectrum.

Obviously, I can't empathize with each of you. I am only one person with limited life experience. But I know you're not alone. I have asked God to speak to your heart through this book—no matter who you are. I pray you will find encouragement in my words even if I've never been in your shoes (or your lingerie, so to speak).

Your View of Sex

Thankfully, I came from a home that viewed sex in a biblical way. My parents saved sex for marriage, though Mom candidly admits they weren't perfect angels. As I grew up, they demonstrated their love to each other in visible ways, which led me to believe (no details, please!) that life behind their bedroom door was most satisfactory.

Mom shared honestly (albeit discreetly) about sex—when I was brave enough to ask—but I also did my share of snooping in her bedroom when she wasn't home. Nothing was safe from my curious adolescent prying—not the box of mail-order condoms in the back of Dad's sock drawer, not the balled-up towel under the bed, not the scandalously sexy lingerie in Mom's bottom dresser drawer.

Embarrassingly enough, I actually used to empty her negligee drawer out onto her bed when I was home alone and put it on piece by piece. I'd pose in front of the mirror and pretend it was my wedding night. I wasn't sure how some of it worked—especially the ones with the dangerous metal clips dangling from the bottom. (She is so going to shoot me when she reads this.)

Mom also had a pair of stiletto heels that I'd seen in her closet, yet I had never seen her wear. Once I caught her slipping them into her suitcase while she was packing for an overnight trip with Dad. I pulled them out by their long, thin, wraparound straps.

"Where are you going to wear *these?*" I asked innocently.

Her flushed face and impish grin gave away the answer. I quickly exited the bedroom and knew I would never look at those shoes the same again.

You might not have grown up in a family that had a healthy view of sex. Perhaps your parents were promiscuous before marriage with disastrous results. Maybe they even encouraged you to be sexually free. Perhaps they showed no signs of loving each other while you were growing up in their home. Maybe you lived with Mom and her latest boyfriend for most of your life. Perhaps you were taught that sex was sinful, dirty, or a necessary evil of marriage.

If you've grown up with the idea that nice girls don't talk (or think) about sex, hopefully this chapter will open your mind and your heart to a different point of view—God's, in fact. Nice girls can think—and even talk—about sex. If your image of a godly woman is one that prohibits any mention of sex, my candidness might make you a bit uncomfortable. But my prayer is that my words will never violate the principles in God's Word.

Scripture is chock-full of references to sensual pleasures that God has created for a woman and her husband to enjoy. Your spirituality and your sexuality are not separate, isolated parts of you. Enjoying sexual, sensual pleasures with your hubby not only pleases God, it even demonstrates obedience to His will for your life.

God's Plan for Sex

God created sex before the fall, so it existed in the perfect world of Eden before sin ever came into the picture.

In her book *Pillow Talk,* Karen Scalf Linamen asks us to consider what was going through God's mind when He created a man and a woman and placed them alone—and completely naked—in the middle of paradise on earth.

"Did he see the way their bodies knit and moved together during lovemaking and muse to himself, 'Now look at what they've gone and done. I certainly didn't have *that* in mind when I gave Adam that there appendage and created those nooks and crannies for Eve.'"[1]

As soon as Genesis finishes explaining how God made woman and how she and the man will leave their parents and cleave to each other, it says, "The man and his wife were both naked, and they felt no shame" (2:25).

Why would He put that in there if He didn't mean for us to be intimate, vulnerable, sensual, and sexual with our mates?

Solomon writes in Proverbs 5:18-19, "May your fountain be blessed, and may you rejoice in the wife of your youth. A loving doe, a graceful deer—may her breasts satisfy you always, may you ever be captivated by her love."

Rejoice. Satisfy. Captivated. These words describe God's plan for your sex life. And we haven't even touched on the Song of Solomon yet—whoa!

God created everything, sex included, and in His perfect plan, everything would work smoothly and beautifully without a hitch. Let's oil our engines and get them up and running—just as God intended!

Did You Wait?

I thank God that when my little girls ask me someday if Daddy and I saved sex for marriage, I will be able to look them in the eyes and say, "Yes, we did." But what if they aren't satisfied with that answer and want to know more? What if they say, "Okay, Mom, so we know what you *didn't* do before marriage, but what *did* you do?"

I'm afraid my face will turn pink and feel warm to the touch. My stomach will churn. I'll swallow hard, say a quick prayer, and tell them the truth.

I won't share details with you at this time, but if I did, many of you might say, "What's the big deal? That's not so bad! You saved all kinds of stuff for marriage—oral sex, intercourse, seeing each other naked…"

Some might even say, "I've done more than that on a first date!"

Even now, I sometimes look back on our premarital physical relationship and think, "We didn't do anything wrong—not really."

But I know I've disappointed the one Person who loves me more than anyone else ever will. When I get to heaven and am held accountable for every wrong thing I've done, I can picture the scene. I look up into Jesus' face, and He asks me (even though He already knows) to tell Him how physically intimate I was before marriage. Tears fill my eyes.

He shakes His head lovingly at me and says, "My child, didn't I tell you I knew what was best for you? Don't you wish you would have saved *everything* for marriage?"

My friend, if you aren't married yet, let me plead with you. Don't let your physical relationship have first place, or a number of things will happen.

1. The more physical you are, the more physical you'll want to be. It will get harder and harder to stop.

2. Talking and getting to know one another won't satisfy you or appeal to you. You won't be happy unless you're touching.

3. You won't know the person you're marrying nearly as well as you think you do—and this will cause much grief later.

4. Your physical relationship after you're married won't be as fulfilling as you had dreamed.

5. God will not be pleased with or honored by your relationship, and you will miss out on so many of His blessings.

God created sex to be beautiful and wonderful in the context of marriage. Satan is the imitator and twister of all that God created as good. He wants you to believe that engaging in sexual activity before you're married won't bring any consequences.

"What's the difference?" he asks. "As long as you're going to marry him, who cares what you do in the weeks and months before your wedding day? What's the big deal?"

Why Wait?

In God's eyes, there is *no bigger deal.* He didn't just throw together some random ideas, call it sex, and start handing it out to humans like cookies—"Eat as many as you'd like, whenever you'd like, with whomever you'd like!"

No, sex is His brilliant, well-planned, only-works-when-you-follow-the-manual creation—a masterpiece.

First Corinthians 6:18-20 explains why sexual sin is the most dishonoring to God. "All other sins a man commits are outside his body, but he who sins sexually sins against his own body. Do you not know that your body is a temple of the Holy Spirit, who is in you…?

You are not your own; you were bought at a price. Therefore honor God with your body."

How do you know whether or not you're honoring God with your body? You aren't going to find any references in the Bible that define the line between what's acceptable and what's not.

The Bible does say that "just because something is technically legal doesn't mean that it's spiritually appropriate. If I went around doing whatever I thought I could get by with, I'd be a slave to my whims" (1 Corinthians 6:12 MSG).

We are technically allowed to do plenty of things that aren't always beneficial to us. When we rush up to that imaginary line and dangle our hands (and other body parts) over it, we're actually giving up our freedom. We become a slave to that line, to sin. We find ourselves unable to keep from crossing the line, so we move it a little. And a little more. That's what I did. We can't stop.

Romans 7:5 (MSG) tells us, "For as long as we lived that old way of life, doing whatever we felt we could get away with, sin was calling most of the shots."

If you are doing everything you think you can get away with physically, sin is calling the shots in your relationship. This is no way to live. True freedom comes from doing what you know in your heart is right.

So where do you draw the line? My honest opinion is that anything the two of you wouldn't feel comfortable doing with someone else in the room, you shouldn't be doing when you're alone.

Would he have his hands up your shirt with your dad sitting beside him? I doubt it. Would you be sprawling on top of each other with his mom watching? I don't think so. Would you sit in a crowded room with his pants unzipped or your shirt lying beside you on the floor? Hmm…

Am I hypocritical for saying that when I didn't follow my own advice? No, just regretful—because I wish I had.

Empty Calories

Empty calories—the kind in junk food—have zero nutritional value. All they're good for is making you full. Or fat. Or sick. Your hunger pangs are quieted, but your body is no better off than before. In fact, you're in worse shape than ever. When you fill up on junk food, you're not hungry for the stuff your body really needs, so you go without it. Sooner or later, you feel the effects.

When your physical relationship gets hot and heavy before marriage, you feel full—as if you were really close to the person. You feel an emotional connection that doesn't really exist. It's an illusion of Satan's. He takes something hollow and shallow, like a physical relationship before marriage, and tries to convince you that it can take the place of an emotional and spiritual connection with your future spouse. Only later do you discover his schemes.

Think of the physical part of your premarital relationship as empty calories. A few bites of junk food a day won't hurt you. Holding hands, a few sweet kisses, some hugs are okay.

But when you start filling up your relationship with potato chips and gummy bears, the fresh fruits and veggies get left out, and your relationship becomes malnourished. Don't let Satan fool you into living on his junk food. It's not worth it.

Accountability

One of my good friends is dating a wise and admirable young man. This couple (let's call them Drew and Julia) met a little over a year ago, and it didn't take long before they knew they wanted to spend the rest of forever together. They attend the same college and make frequent overnight visits to her parents' house on the weekends. They can't get married for another two years. Can you see where this is heading?

You know how it is staying up late to watch a movie together. The room is dark, you're all alone, you're tired, your senses are aroused, your defenses diminished. You're snuggling on the couch, then you're lying down with your head on his lap, then you're lying side-by-side, then on top of each other. Even if you never take off a stitch of clothing, it's easy to cross boundaries and break rules.

Drew has come up with a solution for temptation that has worked so far for him. He and his buddy Jake have a deal. They've drawn the line at kissing their girlfriends—no inappropriate touching—and if they get turned on, they stop. If Drew crosses the line, he owes Jake $50. And vice versa. After each date, they compare notes and pay up if they have to.

Just the other week, Julia shared with me that Drew upped the ante. After a close call with Julia, Drew told Jake that the new penalty would have to be $100. "You can stay at $50 if you want," Drew told Jake, "but it's going to have to be $100 for me."

And since Drew is a poor college student scrimping and saving to buy his girl a nice diamond engagement ring, he can't afford to be making payments like that.

If you and your love are still in the premarital club, I strongly urge you to find an accountability partner to help keep you and your honey pure. I didn't share details of my physical relationship with Gabe with anyone, and I know I would have been better off if I had.

Second Chances

You're married now. The past is behind you. Or is it? What are you supposed to do if you and your husband went too far while you were dating? What if you had sex—a lot? What if you got pregnant? What if you've had an abortion? What if you were sexually active with lots of different guys? What do you do now?

I have a friend who dated a guy in high school and for a couple of years afterward. They became sexually involved—and the sex felt good! When they broke up and she met and married her now-husband, their marriage bed was the source of many problems. She struggled intensely with the lack of attraction and excitement she felt for her husband. She couldn't keep from dwelling on the illicit passion she had shared with another.

My friend has to train her mind to forget her past relationship and focus on her husband. The task is impossible to undertake—on her own. She must daily seek God's help. It won't happen overnight. She'll have to work at it for a long, long time.

The good news is that her God is a God of grace. We will never completely understand how He can forgive us when we repent of our sin. How He can look at us and see the perfection of His Son, Jesus Christ. How He can wash away that kind of filth and stain from our lives and give us second chances left and right. I don't know how He does it except that He's God. He's grace. He's love.

That's the awesome news. The bad news is that we will still feel the consequences of our sins. A woman with a sexual past will struggle more than a woman who was completely pure going into marriage. The past may haunt you every now and again, or every day of your life, depending on how bad it was. But God forgives you! His desire is to cleanse you and forgive you and help you move on to experience His rich blessings of beautiful, wonderful sexual love with your husband.

Dwell on His love and forgiveness. Memorize Scriptures that remind you that Christ's blood has made you white as snow. Meditate on His grace and pray that you will feel it in your heart and soul. Praise Him for giving you another chance to do this right. And thank

Him for the unique opportunity you have to share His grace with other girls struggling with a similar past.

Ask God to cleanse your mind of the past and help you start anew with your husband. Give it time, but expect Him to answer your prayers.

You're Not Alone

So many young married women I surveyed expressed disappointment in their sex lives for various reasons. Many of them were embarrassed by the way they felt.

"What's wrong with me?" they wanted to know. "Everybody else thinks sex is awesome! Why isn't it for me?"

I used to meet some friends for a monthly book club. One night, our topic of conversation turned to sex. One newly wedded friend almost started crying when she found out she wasn't alone.

"I thought something was wrong with me!" she said. "I haven't told anyone about this because I thought no one would understand! I thought when I got married, I'd want sex all the time. This has been killing me inside!"

She was overcome with relief when she discovered she was normal. She wasn't a misfit or a failure. Her problem was common, even among many of her friends.

If all of us women were completely honest, none of us would feel alone. But no one wants to admit that her sex life is blah, or that she has no desire for sex, or that she's never experienced an orgasm. We do, after all, have our pride to consider.

A few weeks ago, my newly married friend Ally put her pride aside and shared some insight on sex with me. She did her best to respect the privacy of her month-old marriage, but she knew I was writing a book for women like her, and she wanted to help.

I asked her to share her biggest disappointment regarding sex.

"Trying to have an orgasm," she replied. "The books say it's just mental, but I don't know."

"It's frustrating too," she added, "because he wants to have sex really late before we go to bed, and I'm so tired. When it doesn't feel good, and it's taking him a long time to orgasm, that's really hard. It's difficult when I'm not in the mood or sex isn't feeling good. He can't enjoy himself unless I force myself to be excited."

Ally's story is one of hundreds like it going on even as I write.

> "Our honeymoon was awful. He was so excited to finally be able to make love to me, and he didn't understand why I wasn't equally thrilled."

> "I didn't realize there would be times I wouldn't be interested in sex. That just made no sense to me in the heat of our dating relationship."

> "Sex is just another thing to fit into my already full schedule. That's terrible, but it's how I feel."

> "Keeping ourselves pure physically when we were dating was so hard. All I thought about was sex. What happened?"

> "We've probably had sex almost 50 times now, and it still hurts!"

Can you relate to any of these so far? I know I could in my first few years of marriage.

> "I'm disappointed that sex isn't fun and exciting like I thought it would be. Our marriage would be so much better if we didn't have to deal with it."

> "We were both virgins when we got married, but we definitely messed around while we were dating. To be honest, messing around felt a lot better than sex does!"

"I usually just end up faking being excited in bed so my husband won't get upset."

"I hate the mess! I'm a neat freak as it is, and I hate it when our sheets get all sweaty and sticky."

"He never wants to talk. All he wants is sex! I don't think he really even cares about me as a person!"

I asked Ally what shocked her most about sex. "How mental it was for me," she said. "I didn't want to do it as often as I thought I would. I was determined not to be like those wives who refused sex for their husbands, and I found out how easily I became one of them."

Why is sex so much different than we thought it would be? I think I know.

See You at the Movies

"I had no idea sex was so messy!" a friend of mine told me. "I was totally shocked!"

"Why in the world didn't someone tell me sex makes a mess?" another young woman asked. "Or is that one of those things we're just supposed to *know*?"

"Nobody told me that what goes up must come down!" one girl stated bluntly. "I didn't realize I'd be leaking for hours afterward!"

And who would? Think about it. Just watch any TV show or movie where two people have any sort of sexual chemistry. They go to dinner, share a drink, take a moonlit stroll through the park, and head to her place.

After the bedroom scene starts to steam up, if it's a PG-rated movie, they immediately skip to the frame where she lazily rolls over in bed, opens her eyes, dreamily pats the bed beside her, only to discover he's gone. The sun streams through the window, casting a glow on the clean, white sheets. There's a note on the pillow—and a rose—which she sensually brings to her lips. She falls back on the pillow, clasps her fingers together, stretches her arms above her head, smiles and sighs. Aaahhh…

And we wonder why newly married women are surprised by the mess. What mess? Pardon my skepticism, but I just have a question or two about Movie Girl and her delicious sexual experience.

First of all, they'd been wearing the same underwear all day. And they didn't take time to freshen up or anything. Do movie people just naturally smell like roses? Do they never have periods? And I really want to know why they didn't lay a towel down on the bed to absorb the dripping and keep those pretty silk sheets from getting stained.

And, uh…since he obviously wasn't wearing a condom—who has time for those pesky things in the heat of the moment?—did she sleep all night in a nice, warm puddle? Or did we miss the part where she ran to the bathroom holding a wad of tissues between her legs? Is there a plausible explanation for her hair being perfectly in place or (at the very least) perfectly tousled and her lipstick looking as fresh as it did eight hours before? I won't bore you with the last ten questions on my list.

Sex isn't all we thought it would be because our expectations weren't based in reality.

Sexpectations

Admit it. One of the most disappointing aspects of your new marriage is the sex. When you were dating, you could hardly keep your hands off each other. You might have saved sex for marriage, but barely.

You probably expected sex for the first time with your husband to be the most erotic and thrilling experience of your life. And you expected it to just keep getting better. How in the world were the two of you going to get anything done? You'd be having sex three, four, five times a day. And wow, would it be hot!

I realize I'm generalizing here, but chances are, you can identify. You expected sex to be one thing. Reality is something entirely different.

Joanne Heim can relate. "Sex didn't turn out to be what I expected," she says. "How could it? I'd built up a fantasy in my mind, never bothered to tell Toben what I was expecting, and forgot to take into account the fact that I'd never done it before and that trying anything for the first time can be difficult."[2]

Karen Linamen comments on this phenomenon, which is common among married women the world over. "Unfortunately," she says, "intimacy, whether of the flesh or of the emotions, never seems to ripen in real life with the fertile ease with which it thrives in our imaginations...For some unknown reason, there seems to exist for most of us a vast chasm between our fantasies and reality—a yawning canyon separating our expectations and our experiences."[3]

Christians Misleading Christians

The secular media aren't the only ones misleading us in the bedroom. We might not have considered another culprit—Christian books about sex. Without meaning to, many of them may have done more harm than good—painting a picture of sex within marriage that is less than realistic. I have found many of them to be lofty and idealistic rather than candid and real.

Why wouldn't I think sex was just naturally going to be phenomenal after reading things like this? "Foreplay can be delightful for both husband and wife, if the husband realizes that his tender skill will prepare his wife for the love act itself."

When two newlyweds are learning how to get along with each other and have sex with each other, they are simultaneously young, immature, inexperienced, and self-centered. Hence, words like *delightful* and *tender* often go flying out the window.

Sex between newly married couples can be passionate, sure, but let's not forget to use words like *clumsy, inconsiderate, smelly,* and *frustrating.* This is not to discourage couples from developing an awesome sex life, but to *encourage* them that they are not alone if these descriptors fit their current sex life better than any others.

"Nobody's sex life is such that every experience is a ten," Dr. Kevin Leman points out. "You may have to be satisfied with regular eights or sixes and even an occasional three."[4] Those are the kinds of reassuring words we need to hear.

The 20-Year Warm-Up

I remember reading, before I was married, that sex is a 20-year warm-up.

"That is just ridiculous," I thought. "In my marriage, sex is going to be hot from day one! To heck with the 20-year warm-up!"

I didn't keep a "sex diary," so I couldn't tell you exactly how good (or bad) it was my first year of marriage. I know it hurt on my honeymoon—all ten days pretty much. We hiked every day in the Smoky Mountains, and I would pray for good weather so we could stay outside as long as possible. Thankfully, we weren't the only hikers around, so Gabe didn't get any ideas about making whoopee on a blanket in the woods.

There were times in the next couple years when sex was really good—and times when it was so-so or even awful. Hit-and-miss, I'd call it. As time goes on, we have more good months than bad, we learn more about what pleases each other, and overall, sex has gotten better. But we have to work at it. It doesn't come naturally. That's the part I didn't expect.

My friend Ally has already picked up on that fact, young as she is.

"It takes a lot of giving and selflessness," she says, "but once I make the effort, the results always turn out great for both of us."

Last month, our life in the bedroom was great. One week in particular was phenomenal. And it was directly related to the time and effort I put into it. I thought about sex, read about sex, bought new lingerie, and spent quality time with my hubby each evening before we headed to the boudoir.

After that sensational month, I was secretly hoping that, from then on, I wouldn't have to work on our sex life anymore. Maybe, just maybe, we had reached a magical plateau in our marriage where splendid sex—effortless sex—was the rule, not the exception. Ha!

That was *last* month. *This* month has been mediocre—even frustrating—and I know exactly why. Sex has taken a backseat to all the other urgent things on my must-do list—like finishing this book manuscript. This book I'm writing about love and marriage and sex. Oh, the irony.

Got Any Advice?

I asked my survey takers to share some helpful advice on sex. Feel free to take it or leave it, but I thought you might be interested in hearing what other Christian women have to say.

> "Don't expect it to be like the movies—perfect the first time!"

> "You don't have to rush it. Snuggling is okay on your wedding night."

> "Sometimes you won't be in the mood, but do it to show hubby you love him."

> "It is great in the morning!"

> "It's better in the afternoon than late at night, for some reason."

"Be open about what you enjoy and what you don't. Sometimes it's just about pleasing the other person."

"Don't compare your sex life to that of others because each couple is different. If both of you are happy and satisfied, don't worry about it."

"It takes time to learn to do it well."

"Your husband will know you love him when you put time, energy, and excitement into it."

"Sometimes it's a little rough in the beginning, but that's normal."

"I was always led to believe it was duty, but with God and a patient husband, I realized it was something to enjoy. Take your time and learn to enjoy it!"

"Always be willing to please your husband so he isn't tempted anywhere else."

"I am the one God designed to meet my husband's sexual needs! What an incredible thought!"

I have one piece of advice of my own to add. Just last week, I found two books on sex I'd heard were good. I asked Gabe if I could order them online, even though our budget was tight.

His reply made me chuckle. "You can spend all the money you want if you're going to get books about sex!"

Do your marriage a favor. Find a good book about sex and read it. For us women, sexual desire isn't there unless we have sex on the brain. And unlike men, thoughts about sex don't always just pop randomly into our heads. We have to make a conscious decision to think about sex. Reading a good Christian book on the topic will increase your desire to make love.

And believe me, your husband will thank you!

You Can Do It!

Sex really does get sweeter with time. That is, if you take the time and effort to cultivate your sexual relationship with your husband. Of course, each individual experience is not going to be better than the one before. Wow—that would be something. But eventually, the rough spots will be ironed out, and the duds will be fewer and further between. It just gets sweeter. If you're willing to make the effort, the 20-year warm-up moniker is right on target as far as I'm concerned.

Your relationship outside of sex is a big factor in how good your sex life is. People say that sex is not a thermostat but a thermometer. You don't turn up the heat in the bedroom. You reflect the heat that's already there. Your growth as a person and a couple will positively affect your experience in bed. This is part of the reason why couples that have been married longer have better sex.

However, if you and your husband have drifted apart emotionally in the months and years since you got married, you're off the path of that 20-year warm-up thing. But the God of grace and healing and restoration can help you get back on that path!

We do have to work at sex—if we want it to be good and keep getting better. But good it can be! And the more you work at becoming a selfless, respectful, loving wife, the better sex will be for you. Ask God to infuse you with desire for your husband, and He will.

Last month, I would have used words like *delightful, phenomenal,* and *thrilling* to describe our tumbles in the hay. If those are the last three words you'd use to describe your sex life right now, don't lose hope! Someday (maybe soon!) those adjectives could be yours!

10

Faithfulness in Action

Drink water from your own cistern, running water
from your own well. Should your springs overflow in the streets, your
streams of water in the public squares?
Let them be yours alone,
never to be shared with strangers.

PROVERBS 5:15-17

I love Bible passages that share truth in analogy form, like the poetic words above. In Solomon's day, wells and cisterns were privately owned and valuable—not unlike marriage.

Proverbs 5 continues—"May your fountain be blessed, and may you rejoice in the wife of your youth. A loving doe, a graceful deer—may her breasts satisfy you always, may you ever be captivated by her love. Why be captivated, my son, by an adulteress? Why embrace the bosom of another man's wife?" (verses 18-20).

We could change the wording a bit and apply those verses to us wives. Are you satisfied with your husband? Are you captivated by his love alone? Do you rejoice in him and no other? Have you been completely faithful in body, mind, and soul?

Of Marriage and Nachos

When Gabe and I were dating, our favorite restaurant was Don

Pablo's. Between the two of us, we had tried a total of one entrée on the menu—chicken nachos. Though everyone around us was ordering all sorts of other south-of-the-border delicacies, we didn't care. We knew what we liked, and why mess with a good thing?

Our delight in chicken nachos is like our single-mindedness in marriage. When Gabe and I got married, we made a lifetime commitment. Regardless of what happens or who else comes along, we will never even "look at the menu."

Someday in the future, I may be tempted to check out other Mexican entrées at Don's, but I pray that God will keep temptation away from our marriage. With His help, forever faithfulness is our goal.

"That's how it is for me too," you're thinking. "I would never dream of being unfaithful to my husband. Shame, shame on anyone who is!"

I'm glad you and I have such firm convictions, but let me share a word of caution straight from Scripture. "If you think you are standing firm, be careful that you don't fall!" (1 Corinthians 10:12). Don't miss the exclamation point. This is important and it's for everyone—especially those of us who *think* we're standing firm.

We often listen to gossip of other people's extramarital affairs and feel a bit smug. Overconfident in our ability to resist sin.

The Message says, "Don't be so naive and self-confident. You're not exempt. You could fall flat on your face as easily as anyone else."

"Contrary to popular belief, fidelity and commitment are not practiced by the passive act of not doing something," Karen Scalf Linamen warns.[1]

It's not enough to just not have an affair. We have to take an active stance against infidelity. We need to be faithful by *design,* not *default.*

How do we do this? Pray for God's hedge of protection around our marriages—even when things are going well. Prevention is key.

Satan wants us to think it can't happen to us. He's just waiting for us to stop praying about it so he can jump in and take over. Let's foil his evil plans.

Lust Redefined

We'll start by talking about lust. I don't struggle much with lust—as long as we're using the traditional definition of the word. Lust—to stare at an attractive man I'm not married to and imagine having sex with him. Not my cup of tea.

But what if lust isn't limited to such a narrow definition? In the dictionary, lust is more generally defined as an intense longing. Women are more emotionally than sexually driven, and lust for us can take a different form. Have you ever lusted *emotionally?* I know I have.

Ever looked at someone else's husband and thought how much easier or exciting your life would be if your husband were more like him? Ever felt an "intense longing"—no matter how brief—for your hubby to have one or more of the qualities you see in another man? That smacks of lust.

You don't want your hubby staring at another woman and wishing you *looked* like her. So you shouldn't be looking at another man and wishing your husband *acted* like him. If I don't want Gabe drooling over another woman's big breasts or long legs, then I shouldn't be drooling over another man's spirituality or romantic nature.

"So-and-so's husband is so much more patient, considerate, spiritual, poetic, loving…"—you fill in the blank. We've all said it—or at least thought it.

Jesus says that someone who lusts after a man she's not married to has already committed adultery in her heart (Matthew 5:28). Do you squirm when you look at lust in this light? We can try to rationalize our behavior, but it won't do any good.

Faithful in Every Way

"At one point in time, I was having an affair with five different men." I read these words in a Christian magazine, and my jaw dropped to my boobs.

The author went on to explain that she had not actually had affairs with her coach, professor, pastor, neighbor, and coworker, but she'd been fantasizing about the desirable character qualities and physical attributes they possessed. What her husband lacked, she found in these men.

Comparing your husband to other men is like a gangrene that eats away at the insides of your marriage. It can quickly lead you down a road that will destroy your relationship with your husband.

Do you find yourself thinking, "I wish my husband were more like him?" When you have thoughts like these, the key is to not dwell on them. Distract yourself. Change the subject on yourself.

Better yet, pray. "God, take this thought far away from me. Get behind me, Satan. Flee!" The initial thought is not a sin, but prolonging that thought is. The same goes for a second look or a "harmless" daydream.

Picture this: Your church's worship leader gets up in front to pray. You notice his new haircut. His shirt and tie complement his eyes perfectly. Your husband hates ties.

You watch him flash a quick smile at his wife before he prays and wonder why your husband is never that affectionate toward you. He's so eloquent when he prays. Your husband mumbles.

Stop! Stop at the haircut. Think of something else—like your husband. Or the words of the worship song. Ask God to help you focus on Him.

Satan knows our weaknesses, and he's going to put temptations in our path when and where we're most likely to succumb to them. He's no dummy.

The reason God allows us to be tempted is not that He wants us to give in. He wants us to show that we love Him enough to put His commands over our sinful, fleshly desires. He promises to always provide a way out of temptation but doesn't promise it will be easy (1 Corinthians 10:13).

When you successfully defeat temptation, the Lord rejoices and blesses you. James 1:12 (MSG) says, "Anyone who meets a testing challenge head-on and manages to stick it out is mighty fortunate. For such persons loyally in love with God, the reward is life and more life."

The key to defeating temptation is to be so "loyally in love with God" that you seek Him and desire Him more than any sin, regardless of how alluring it may be.

Guard Your Eyes and Heart

It's not just real-life people you need to guard your eyes and heart against. There was a time in the not-too-distant past when I faithfully watched a certain sitcom every Thursday night. The characters were sexy, funny, and intriguing. I could hardly wait to see what would happen next in their lives. The thought of missing an episode was devastating. When I caught myself saying, "Only five more days until Thursday," I knew I was addicted.

So I stopped cold turkey. No more Thursday night date with the boob tube (quite an appropriate moniker, eh?). It wasn't much fun at first. The urge to turn to NBC at 7:58 (couldn't miss the theme song!) was strong.

After a couple weeks, my craving started to diminish. After a month, I had forgotten about the show completely. Even now, when I'm tempted to watch a rerun (they don't count, right?), I end up turning the channel. I enjoy my freedom too much.

We think we can watch sleazy sitcoms and reality shows without

our minds being polluted. "It's not like *I'm* living that way," we rationalize. "I just like to be entertained by people who are."

Watching these shows desensitizes us to sin. What harm is there
really in drinking, sexual innuendos, flirting with married men, coarse
joking, lying, kissing a different guy every weekend? Subconsciously,
we begin to think of it as an acceptable lifestyle.

Television also handicaps our husbands. We eat up the romance
and passion portrayed on TV, compare it with our own lives, and
resent our husbands for not providing us with such a fairy-tale existence. But the guys in the sitcoms have an unfair advantage over
our "commonplace" husbands. We see their white teeth, perfect hair,
rippling muscles, sense of humor, and fashion savvy, but we don't
experience their bad breath, bad hair days, and bad moods. If we do,
those things are just written into the script as charming, endearing
little quirks.

We can forget that these actors aren't real people. Our husbands
are. And whether you realize it or not, you'll start to compare your
husband to these guys, and he won't be able to compete.

My friend Jodie says, "Just like 'you are what you eat,' we become
what we watch and listen to. Jason and I try to be very selective. We
don't want Satan to destroy our gift of companionship."

What Not to Wear

What you put in your mind is important, but so is what you put
on your body. Are you ever guilty of dressing to draw attention to
specific parts of your figure? Are you subtly (or not so subtly) flaunt-
ing your best features in order to get men to take notice? Are your
skirts too short, your tops too low, your pants and shirts too snug?

Just the other day, I read about a test you can do if you're wondering if your T-shirt is too tight. Put it on, and with your finger, press
down on the area between your breasts Then let go. If it bounces

back like a rubber band, guess what—too tight. How many of your shirts would fail the rubber band test?

Or how about the roller coaster test? Lift your arms in the air like you're flying down a hill at 90 mph. Does your belly show? Time to buy some longer shirts.

And don't even get me started on the lingerie everyone is wearing in public these days, peeking out under blazers and button-down shirts.

We can usually tell when something is inappropriate. If it's the slightest bit questionable, choose something else. The object isn't to see what you can get away with.

We dress a certain way because we crave that rush we get when guys notice us. They don't glance twice at the girls wearing regular clothes. You've got to have low-riding jeans that hug your hips and rear and that tight shirt that shows off your belly button and molds to your body.

I know how hard it is to find clothes these days that are both fashionable and decent. I'm five feet, ten inches tall with long legs, a really long torso, a small chest, a round bottom, and the hips of a woman who has birthed two babies.

No one makes cute shirts that cover my belly button. Or one-piece bathing suits that fit my torso and my cup size both. Or jeans that reach my ankles and cover my rear end simultaneously. Or sundresses that hide my underwear, let alone reach my knees.

I can't count the times I've gone shopping for these items and come home frustrated and empty-handed.

Yes, dressing in a modest, Christ-pleasing way might require some sacrifice from time to time. But it is doable. There *are* clothes out there for you—you just have to look a little harder. You might not always get to wear the latest fashions if they're immodest or indecent. You'll have to do without the admiring glances from the men. But you'll be okay.

Girl, you don't need this kind of attention from men to feel good about who you are—especially if you're married! Feel good about the fact that you're strong enough to stand against the temptation to give in to the culture around you. You know what really matters in life. You're more than a sex object—you're a complete woman. You find your self-worth in Jesus Christ, not from the attention of men you aren't even married to.

Don't ruin your testimony as a follower of Christ or hinder your marriage by dressing in a way that isn't pleasing to the Lord.

I'm not advocating baggy turtlenecks and shapeless, floor-length khaki skirts. I'm not saying you can't wear anything that flatters your figure or makes you look attractive. By all means, dress attractively in clothes that fit you well. Wear your hair and makeup in a way that is flattering to your face. But use common sense and good judgment, honoring Christ and your husband.

A few women have mentioned to me that their husbands are part of the problem. They don't mind their wives dressing suggestively and even suggest that they do. Some husbands get kicks out of dangling their prize in front of other men and watching them squirm. Not cool.

I believe in submitting to your husband as long as his requests don't contradict God's Word. Pray that God will speak to his heart and convict him not to pressure you to do something that is immoral or, at the very least, uncomfortable for you.

You don't have to dress provocatively to look beautiful—you already are a prize.

Is It *His* Fault?

Christian men are not exempt from the struggle with visual temptation and mental sexual sin. A man's autonomic nervous system is controlled by his environment—what he sees. He isn't capable of controlling it himself. (Hence the prefix "auto.")

A pretty woman with suggestive clothing walks by, and the guy's brain, chemicals, blood, pulse, and temperature all kick into gear automatically. Sure, he can override this reaction with godly thoughts and prayers for help, but it's not an easy task. Is this something you want to be a part of—causing a godly man to stumble?

A woman I know (who tends to dress suggestively) once told me that she's sick and tired of women getting blamed for men's failure to control themselves. "It's not fair that I can't wear what I want just because men are perverts!" she said.

If that's your mind-set, I encourage you to do some actual scientific research. As I just mentioned, a man is not physically capable of preventing that kind of reaction in his body. He can push it away when it comes. He can remove himself from the situation. He can plead and pray with God to distract his mind. But he cannot help his body's initial reaction to a beautiful woman and her body.

And though some men may struggle with this more than others, you might be surprised to find that it affects godly and ungodly men alike. It's not reserved for "perverts."

If you find yourself agreeing with this woman, take a minute to think about what you're saying. Why do you wear tight, low, or skimpy clothing in the first place? If you're honest, it's so that men will be attracted to your body. Can you reasonably expect men to find your body parts *attractive* (especially your breasts and rear end) without thinking anything *sexual* about them?

That's like asking, "Why can't he just appreciate my cleavage in a *pure* way?" Um, okay.

The apostle Paul is famous for his warnings to Christians about not causing our brothers and sisters in Christ to stumble in any way.

He doesn't particularly mention low-cut tops and low-riding jeans (obviously), but the principle still applies.

"So whether you eat or drink or whatever you do, do it all for the glory of God," Paul says. "Do not cause anyone to stumble" (1 Corinthians 10:31-32).

In Romans 14:13, he challenges us to be as purposeful as possible in this whole stumbling matter. "Make up your mind," he says, "not to put any stumbling block or obstacle in your brother's way." In other words, "Don't get in the way of someone else, making life more difficult than it already is" (MSG). We should be clearing the path to godliness for the guys around us, not putting up obstacles all over the place.

As Christian women getting dressed each morning, we need to "make up our minds" to choose an outfit that has something other than "stumbling block" written all over it. In fact, we should toss out any articles of clothing that could be deemed questionable so we don't have to give a second thought to the statement we're making. Feel free to declare that you are classy or feminine or even fabulous. Just steer clear of "look at my body and lust."

When we dress provocatively or even borderline immodestly, we're not being fair to Christian men who are trying their darnedest to live for Christ in our sick and polluted culture. Instead of encouraging our brothers' growth in Christ, we're acting as hindrances to their faith. That's not only selfish, it's sinful.

On a more positive note, we can replace our selfish ways with behavior that uplifts and edifies our brothers in Christ. Let's commit to finding ways to put them first, to serve them, rather than potentially tempt them.

"Let us therefore make every effort to do what leads to peace and to mutual edification," Paul tells us in Romans 14:19. "For I am not seeking my own good but the good of many" (1 Corinthians 10:33).

Treat others in a way that draws attention to *them,* not you. You can do this by listening more than you talk, by offering words of encouragement, by praying for the growth and purity of your fellow Christians. All of these wonderful "edifiers" prove much more effective without the distraction of inappropriate apparel.

The Best Kind of Clothing

While we're talking about what *not* to wear, let me share something the Bible says we *should* be putting on each day. Colossians 3:12 tells us to clothe ourselves with compassion, kindness, humility, gentleness, and patience. These are "outfits" we can wear for everyone but especially for our husbands.

Notice that these garments aren't attention grabbers. They're plain, simple, quiet, classic pieces in our wardrobe. But when you put them on—*wow!*—what a statement they make to your husband! Your clothing says a lot about you, but these are the clothes that really count.

What reaction would you get from your husband if you got all dressed up in these clothes tomorrow morning? Would he say, "Okay, what do you want from me?" or "Who are you, and what have you done with my wife?" Hopefully, his reaction wouldn't be quite this extreme because you've actually demonstrated these qualities in the past.

I love 1 Peter 3:3-4—"Your beauty should not come from outward adornment…Instead, it should be that of your inner self, the unfading beauty of a gentle and quiet spirit, which is of great worth in God's sight." I want unfading beauty, don't you?

Your true beauty should come from inside you. Pretty is as pretty does. Pair that with an attractive outward appearance, and the total package is spectacular. Do your best with the physical features God has given you, but give the most time and attention to the beauty of the spirit *inside* your body.

Trusting My Husband

Speaking of beauty, there we stood in our wedding finery, knife in hand, seconds away from the ceremonious cutting of the cake.

"Please don't shove it my face, Gabe," I pleaded under my breath.

"I won't," he whispered back.

"Do you *promise?*" I had to know.

"I *promise,*" was his reply.

I heard the words but still felt uneasy. With good reason.

We made the cuts and each took a piece. I knew something was awry when he avoided my eyes, but there was no time to escape. Cake in hand, he smeared it all over my face, showing no mercy. Promise broken.

I chased after him in my dress and heels and flung the cake in the air. It hit him in the back. Then I caught him and plastered his face with icing, to everyone's delight.

This is a silly example, but many wives are forced to face the sad reality of broken promises. Are you afraid to trust your husband? Many women who responded to my survey shared this struggle.

One woman who had been married about a year wrote, "I had to overcome some insecurity and jealousy concerning some of my husband's past relationships. We had a lot of fights at first, but then I had to realize that my husband chose to be with *me* and I could trust him."

Some women realize that their insecurity is a mental thing and learn to overcome it. Others have good reason not to trust their husbands.

One friend of mine painfully endured her husband's unfaithfulness at one point in her marriage. "It has taken a long time to rebuild that trust," she says. "We're still not quite there. I wouldn't wish this on anyone."

If you have faced the awful pain and devastation of your husband's adultery, my heart breaks for you. I pray that God will restore and heal you and your marriage. I know that the path will be long and hard.

I was encouraged by one young woman who shared, "In the beginning, I was insecure and jealous. That caused trouble in my soul. I have learned to trust God for my security in all areas of life." Whether or not your husband is ever unfaithful to you, he will let you down at some point. But even when he does, God won't. This woman learned to put her trust in the only solid Rock.

How thankful we should be that we have a God we can trust, who will never break a promise. "For great is his love toward us, and the faithfulness of the LORD endures forever" (Psalm 117:2).

Tempting Thoughts

What if your husband isn't the one who can't be trusted? What if it's *you?* What if you find yourself giving in to temptation, compromising your fidelity?

When I was little, my grandma always kept her cupboards and freezers filled with goodies that were ours for the asking, but my cousins and siblings and I thought that sneaking treats without permission was more of an adventure. I like to think of it as the "forbidden fruit phenomenon."

My cousin Kelly reminisces a recurring scene from our past. "I so vividly remember throwing spoons into the laundry chute and then sneaking into the basement and stealing bites of ice cream," she says. "If we had asked Grandma, we could have had 29 bowls apiece. But eating stolen ice cream from Grandma's basement is much more exciting than boring old upstairs-freezer ice cream eaten in honesty."

What is it about forbidden fruit that makes it so sweet? It's one of Satan's little tricks. When it comes to sin, Satan doesn't want us to see the whole picture. When we're attracted to another man physically or emotionally, all Satan wants us to notice is that daydreaming about this man, being with this man, even kissing or touching him, would be sinfully delicious. The consequences get pushed to the back of our minds.

James 1:14-15 tells us that our own desires are what drive us to sin. "But each one is tempted when, by his own evil desire, he is dragged away and enticed. Then, after desire has conceived, it gives birth to sin; and sin, when it is full-grown, gives birth to death."

Adultery starts with desire. Desire starts in our thoughts. No wonder Paul tells us to fit "every loose thought and emotion and impulse into the structure of life shaped by Christ" (2 Corinthians 10:5 MSG).

Author Jill Savage shares candidly about a time when she had an emotional affair with another man. She was working as a waitress at a dinner theater to help make ends meet. She began to look forward to work because she liked her dance partner, Mike.

"I enjoyed our playful banter," she says, "our mutual love for music, and even the physical closeness we shared on the stage." Her husband was busy and didn't have much time for her, and she began to justify and rationalize her actions based on her feelings.

"One day," she shares, "a bit of conscience began to eat away at me. I glimpsed at the road of destruction I was walking on. I knew it wasn't right and that I couldn't continue in this direction without causing great harm to our family."[2] She summoned all her courage and told her husband about her feelings. They talked, cried, sought counseling, and found healing in their marriage.

We are engaged in a battle for our thoughts. Satan wants to control them, and we simply cannot let him. "For though we live in the world, we do not wage war as the world does. The weapons we fight with are not the weapons of the world. On the contrary, they have divine power to demolish strongholds" (2 Corinthians 10:3-4).

We have the power to stop the devil in his tracks.

Run!

What do we do when we're faced with temptation? The Old Testament's Joseph is a shining example.

"One day [Joseph] went into the house to attend to his duties, and none of the household servants was inside. [Potiphar's wife] caught him by the cloak and said, 'Come to bed with me!' But he left his cloak in her hand and ran out of the house" (Genesis 39:11-12).

When Potiphar's wife tempted Joseph, he didn't stick around and try to reason his way out of it. He fled! When we find ourselves in a tempting or compromising situation, we should do the same.

First Corinthians 6:18 is a simple exhortation to "flee from sexual immorality." Not walk away, or saunter away, or stay for a while and then leave, but flee!

Remove yourself from a tempting situation as soon as humanly possible, Karen Scalf Linamen strongly urges. Get out of the car. Get out of the room. Get off the phone. Find a different church. A new job. A new circle of friends.

"Woe to the man or woman who expects that he or she can play with fire and not walk away blistered or scarred," she says. "Don't give temptations a chance to flame. Douse them immediately before they become too hot to handle."[3]

Remember When...?

In the past, when I broke up with old boyfriends, I would destroy all evidence that we had ever been a couple. I ripped pictures and letters to shreds and tossed teddy bears and other gifts into the trash. I had a friend in college who broke up with his girlfriend, tore up all her letters and photos, and dumped them in the campus lake.

Why are we so set on destroying this evidence? Frankly, we don't want any visual reminders of a time when we were affectionate toward someone other than our spouse.

If we throw away these unwelcome parts of our history with such force, we should be cherishing our past with our *spouse* with equal gusto. I suggest that you relive your engagement, your wedding, your honeymoon, and other special moments. This helps build a protective hedge around your marriage. A hedge of faithfulness.

Take time to look at old photos, watch your wedding video, or take a trip back to the spot where you had your first date. Write down the story of your engagement or tales from your honeymoon. Your stories don't have to be anything spectacular. Most of our lives aren't thrilling enough to be made into a movie.

We can't live in the past, of course, but your history with your spouse can give hope, meaning, and purpose to the present and your future together. When your marriage seems humdrum, stale, shaky, or even troubled, sometimes a glance back into your past together can breathe new life into your relationship.

Dr. Tim Alan Gardner, in his book *Sacred Sex,* offers this advice: "If you're struggling with what to do to rekindle love, joy, passion, and intimacy in your marriage, I encourage you to heed the advice that Christ gave to the church at Ephesus: 'Do the things that you did at first' (Revelation 2:5)."

Jesus is speaking to a group of believers whose love for Him has grown cold. In essence, He's telling them to go back in time to when they first fell in love with their Savior and start living their lives as they were living them then.

"The advice applies to marriage as well," Dr. Gardner says. "When you first fell in love with your mate, it wasn't because you tripped over a box of chocolates. It was because you were *doing things* that created love."[4]

Author and pastor Tommy Nelson shares similar words of wisdom in his book *The Book of Romance*. He explains that romance dies when we forget just how precious our mate is. Romance requires great care and focus—and doing things with intention.

"It requires that each person keep in active memory what gave birth to the marriage," he says. "It requires that each person continue to remember the special traits in the spouse that fueled attraction at the initial stages of their relationship."[5]

Your Hubby, Your Playmate

Ever heard the saying "All work and no play makes Jack a very dull boy"? We all need to take time to rest and relax—our husbands in particular. If you're like me, you're guilty of pressuring your husband to work, work, work, and do, do, do.

Men desperately need times of refreshing and restoration. If they don't have those times, temptations become a real danger, and burnout is inevitable. Even though we're grown-ups with adult responsibilities, we need to spend time just having fun together.

Playing with our husbands can express our desire for intimacy with them. It can open up new avenues of communication. At the very least, it helps us lighten up, to let down our guard. Something is special about fun and innocent play with your husband. The kind of play that doesn't lead to sex—at least not directly. It's characterized by lots of laughter and silliness, imagination and a sense of adventure. It's fresh, exciting, and spontaneous. It's something my marriage has lacked in the past, and I've determined to change that in the future.

Go swimming in the middle of the night. Go horseback riding—on the same horse. Build a snow fort together. Play in the mud or jump in puddles. Roll down a hill—and then try it while hugging. Play video games. Skip rocks. Feed ducks together—or birds, squirrels, or goats. Climb up on the roof to watch the sunset. Fly a kite.

Play Scrabble or Monopoly. Go on a picnic. Run through a sprinkler. Spin quarters or build a house out of playing cards.

We really don't need to be so serious all the time. How's this for a new motto—"Hard work with plenty of play make (insert hubby's name here) run home to his wife each day!"

Love Is a Battlefield

Speaking of fun and games, have you ever played Capture the Flag? When I was a camp counselor, it was one of my favorite activities.

We divided into two teams—half of the woods belonged to one team and the other half was the opponent's territory. Each team would keep some people back on their side to guard their own flag and send the rest into enemy territory to try to capture the other team's flag. The object was to carry the flag back to your own side without getting tagged by the enemy.

Think of your marriage as the flag. Sometime after you met, you captured your man's attention and, after a while, won his heart. Now you're married. He's yours. But you can't let down your guard. You aren't safe until you escape enemy territory with your flag intact. And it won't be easy!

All along the way, you have enemies who want that flag—they're lurking behind bushes, waiting in ambush, laying traps, even chasing after you in full view. You must guard your flag with your life!

Some enemies will try a different tactic—they'll attempt to get you to forget about your flag and join their side. It sure takes a lot less effort than keeping a struggling marriage alive.

In the game, you can rest easy once you've passed through enemy territory and crossed over to the other side. In real life, this whole life on earth is enemy territory. When can you let down your guard? Not before heaven. You need to guard your marriage—and your heart and mind—with your very life.

Affair-Proofing Your Marriage

I asked Gabe the other day what I could do to help ensure that he was never tempted to be unfaithful to me. "I don't know…" he said. "Initiate sex more?" I'm sure he's not the only husband who feels that way.

In a perfect world, our husbands would be faithful regardless of what we did or failed to do. And sometimes, when a husband has an affair, his wife couldn't have done anything to prevent it. She was godly, attentive, loving, and unselfish, but he still gave in to a temptation he shouldn't have.

We may not be able to totally affair-proof our marriages, but most of us can do more than we're currently doing. We need to cover our marriages in prayer, guard our hearts and minds, and ask God to guard our husbands.'

We need to do all we can to make sure our husbands are sexually fulfilled at home so they're not tempted to look elsewhere. Every wife has two options. Either *she* will have a love affair with her husband, or someone else will come along who will. If you're neglecting sex, for whatever reason, you're putting your marriage at risk.

When lightning strikes a tree in a dry forest, flames soon engulf acres of trees. But forests in wetter climates can withstand lightning strikes much easier. Strong Christian marriages aren't exempt from lightning strikes, "but if the marriages are heavily watered with an unwavering commitment to please God above everything else, the conditions won't be ripe for a devastating fire to follow the lightning strike."[6]

One great way to invest in your marriage is to attend a marriage seminar together as Gabe and I did last spring. We spent two nights in a nice hotel and ate lots of yummy food. The speakers were real, personal, and funny. The atmosphere was light and fun—but we learned a lot too. Anyone I've talked to has said it was worth every penny.

Water your marriage with love, affection, hard work, faithfulness, and commitment—every single day. And don't just water it—drench it, soak it! When that lightning strikes, your marriage will survive!

Part Six

Building Your Home

11

That Woman from Proverbs 31

*She watches over the affairs of her household and
does not eat the bread of idleness.*

PROVERBS 31:27

Lazy. Unmotivated. Sluggard. That was me a few short months after our wedding. I hated housework, so I let it go. The dishes piled up until I ran out of counter space. I only brought out the Lemon Pledge after I lost my knickknacks in the dust. I didn't remember what my bed looked like made or when I had last cleaned the bathroom.

"What is my problem?" I asked myself out loud one afternoon. You'd think I was serving a death sentence every time I had to stick my hands in dishwater or scrub the tub. I moaned and complained and even cried a time or two.

Some Applause, Please

It's not like I never had to do chores growing up. I remember standing on a chair to dry dishes because I was too small to reach the sink. I recall sweeping and mopping the floor, even carting the kitchen chairs into another room in order to do my job as thoroughly as possible. Why such a bad attitude now?

Then I figured it out. As a kid, I got *paid* for my chores! Twenty-five cents an hour! Or was it per chore? No matter what my salary, I had been on a mission to save up my nickels and dimes for something or other that I just *had* to have. That was my drive, my inspiration. As a grown-up married woman, that motivation was missing.

No one was going to step up and offer to pay me to do this house-work. I simply had to come to terms with that fact. Even if Gabe had shelled out a quarter for each completed chore, I doubt it would have helped.

I also remembered the praise Mom gave me for a job well done. Could it be that I was addicted to approval much like the Phari-sees of old who only did good works when they could be seen and applauded by others?

Gabe wasn't ungrateful—he just wasn't very observant. He might notice things like a three-inch ring of grime around the bathtub, but a newly mopped kitchen floor rarely caught his attention. I needed some recognition, some laud and honor!

At that point, I knew I needed some assistance outside myself, so I got on my knees and told the Lord I was desperate. "I know this is a dumb request," I told Him, "and I don't even *want* to request it, but *please* make me a better homemaker!"

I felt God prompting me to open my Bible to Proverbs 31. Great. Just who I wanted to hear about right then—the queen mother of housekeeping!

The List of Standards

I started with verse 10—"A wife of noble character who can find?" Well, if I don't dig too deep into the meaning of "noble," I could pass myself off as such. If she's so tough to find, what am I worried about anyway?

"Worth far more than rubies?" Oh, definitely. Gabe doesn't even like jewelry.

Moving on to verse 11—"Her husband has full confidence in her." Uh...*full* confidence? Like, all the time?

What about verse 12? "She brings him good, not harm, all the days of her life." What about all the times I've criticized Gabe, belittled him, corrected him, given him the silent treatment, purposely aggravated or irritated him? That's an awful lot of harm. I don't suppose the good things cancel the bad ones out.

Verse 13 talks about "working with eager hands." I do this on my own pet projects, but I'd imagine this is referring to work around the house.

"She gets up while it is still dark." Yeah, only if I have to pee.

"She provides food for her family." Do frozen pizzas count?

"And portions for her servant girls." That's what I need! A servant girl!

"She sets about her work vigorously." If you have an uncommonly loose interpretation of "vigorously," maybe.

I skipped the next few verses. All that stuff about spindles and distaffs and making linen garments to sell—I didn't even know how to sew!

Verse 25 says this woman can laugh at the days to come. That would require confidence that God will meet my needs.

Verse 27 is a real kicker—she "does not eat the bread of idleness." I was eating that lazy bread left and right. Italian, pumpernickel, rye—I was chowing down.

And the last verse. Finally. I couldn't take much more. "Give her the reward she has earned." *Earned?* You mean they aren't just passing them out to everyone? Shoot.

If you struggle with keeping your home sparkling and clean, take it to the Lord in prayer. Ask Him to give you the desire and motivation to make your home a calm, clean, clutter-free haven for you and your husband. Ask Him to help you resist laziness and be a good steward of what He has given you.

I'm more motivated when I remember that I'm doing my housework for God. A janitor for Jesus—that's me! (Although I'm amazed He hasn't fired me by now.)

Is She for Real?

If you don't believe in the Bible, then the Proverbs 31 woman is nothing more than a cruel joke to you. But if you believe the Bible is truth, then her presence in the book of Proverbs must serve some purpose. But what?

It doesn't have to mean this chick was *real,* does it? Some think the woman from Proverbs 31 is just a model for us to follow, not a real person. Others suggest she might be a composite of characteristics from several different women.

My opinion? I think she's real. But I'm willing to bet she wasn't born this way. I'm sure that only after time and perseverance through trial was she qualified to serve as a timeless role model for Christian women around the world.

In other words, I don't think she was in her first year of marriage when Proverbs 31 was written. Probably not even in her fifth or tenth year. And I know for a fact she didn't have any nursing infants at the time.

This wonderful lady's traits are something for us to aim for, but we shouldn't beat ourselves up every time we fall short.

Sara's Story

I know a woman who comes awfully close to the amazing gal in Proverbs 31. I met her four years ago while coaching her daughter's sixth-grade basketball team.

I felt an instant connection with Sara. I was immediately drawn to her warm smile, sassy sense of humor, and friendly spirit. She had an uncanny way of making you feel like her sister. I was in awe of her down-to-earth demeanor.

Sara's husband was a well-known athlete, recently retired from a successful professional career. She had every reason (in the world's eyes) to hold her head a little higher than the rest of us, but she didn't. I later learned that she reads Proverbs 31 every day, holding as her standard the virtuous woman in that famous chapter.

To me, Sara embodies all that Proverbs 31 calls women to be—looking after the affairs of her household, rejoicing when her husband succeeds, and an amazing success in her own right. Her life has not been easy, yet she remains strong in her faith and true to her Lord. She has shared with me spiritual insights, parenting and marriage advice, and lots of encouragement.

Just a few months after I met Sara, we moved away, but she and I kept in touch. Last September, we visited Sara and her family and stayed in her home. Up close and personal, she was all I had hoped she would be.

Then the day after Christmas this past year, we received the heart-breaking news that Sara's husband went home to be with the Lord suddenly and unexpectedly. Through her grief and suffering, I have full confidence that Sara will continue to bring honor to her husband, even as she continues life's journey without him by her side.

Thank you, Sara, for being a role model to me. You are a true Proverbs 31 woman.

ABCs

When I was growing up, my mom was an incredible example to me of the woman in Proverbs 31. She would scoff at me saying that because she and I both know she didn't keep the cleanest house on the block. She wasn't big on organizing and didn't bring in extra income from a job or hobby. She couldn't even sew!

But she did (and still does) two things that are the most important of all. (1) She brings good, not harm, to her husband all the days of her life, and (2) she fears the Lord and is to be praised.

If you don't get the hang of even half of Proverbs 31, at least remember the two main points. Fear the Lord and love your husband with all your heart.

Each line of Proverbs 31:10-31 begins with a successive letter of the Hebrew alphabet. I tried my hand at poetry and made my own ABC acrostic about loving my husband. If you're feeling ambitious, give it a go yourself. The writing part is easy. It's the *doing* part that takes work!

Affirm him daily.

Be his biggest cheerleader.

Count the blessings I have in our marriage.

Don't criticize him.

Encourage his hobbies.

Fight for his reputation.

Give him my body, mind, and heart.

Help him with a project he wants to finish.

Inspire him to chase after his dreams.

Just gaze at him adoringly.

Kiss him all over his face and neck.

Love him in spite of his weaknesses.

Make sure he knows he's the only one I'll ever want.

New nighties never hurt!

Offer to rub his feet after a long day.

Pray for the needs dearest to his heart.

Quit nagging!

Remember why I fell in love with him.

Stay committed and faithful to him.

Take the initiative when it comes to sex.

Understand where he's coming from.

View him through God's eyes.

Write him a love letter.

X-amine my own heart daily.

Yearn for God and His Word.

Zealously protect my marriage.

The Proverbs 32 Woman

I always wondered what Proverbs 31 would have looked like if it had been written about me. A pretty scary thought. Let's imagine for a moment that you and I are the heroines in Proverbs' last chapter.

> A wife of average character, who can find? It's not too hard—she's everywhere! She is worth slightly less than rubies. She ranks just a smidge lower than a sports car, big screen TV, and the newest laptop.

Her husband has a fair amount of confidence in her, except when it comes to spending his money and having a hot meal ready when he gets home from work.

She brings him good, not harm, about 250 days a year—give or take a few.

She selects new furniture and yet another pair of shoes she doesn't need and shops with eager eyes.

She is like the merchant ships, bringing her purchases in from malls all over the state.

She gets up as late as she can while still making it to work on time and keeps waffles in the freezer for her husband in case he's hungry enough to make himself breakfast.

She briefly considers an outfit and buys it on her department store credit card. And out of her earnings, she buys even more.

She sets about her housework when she gets around to it (which hasn't been much at all lately). She has exercise equipment in the basement to make her arms strong for her tasks but hasn't had the time or the desire to use it.

She sees that her shopping is profitable, and she falls asleep with the lamp on.

In her hand, she holds a bag of potato chips and grasps the remote with greasy fingers.

She opens her arms to her cat and extends her hands to her family (except for the sister she's not speaking to at the moment).

When it snows, she gets frustrated. The kids are home from school!

She makes her bed—sometimes. She is clothed in the latest fashions and the hottest name brands.

Her husband is respected at work and church where he takes his seat among the other leaders in the community.

She makes scrapbooks and homemade birthday cards and supplies the Pampered Chef and Arbonne party hosts with scads of money.

She is clothed with expensive outfits and leather jackets and laughs at those whose taste in clothing isn't up to par.

She speaks without thinking, and the latest gossip is on her tongue.

She watches over the affairs of her household (when she's not busy watching reality TV) and nibbles on (okay, devours) the cheesecake of idleness.

Her children arise and call, "Hey, where's my baseball uniform?" and her husband also—"Hey, where'd you put my golf clubs?"

Many women do great things, and you're not so bad yourself.

Charm is desirable and beauty is everything, and fearing the Lord is a nice added touch, if you can squeeze it in.

Present to her the Community Service award and the Best-Dressed at the Office award and all those other awards she has earned that mean so much in light of eternity.

Did you see yourself in any of those "verses?" I recognized myself way too often. My prayer is to become less and less like this woman and more and more like the *real* Proverbs 31 woman every day.

His and Hers

Do you ever find yourself looking for a whole chapter of Proverbs devoted to men and their household responsibilities? More than once, I have found myself lamenting in the manner of young children, "It's not fair!"

I once had a class of third graders comment on who has it easier—boys or girls.

"Boys have it easier because they don't have to stay home with children," one boy said. "They don't keep the house clean."

"Boys have it easier because the girls have to do the dishes," said another, "and the laundry and clean the house, and the boys have to watch TV. That's their chore."

The way you and your husband divide up the household chores is none of my business. If hubby's only chore is watching TV and you're okay with that, then that's great. The important thing is that you come up with a plan you can both live with happily.

Before my friend Jodie married Jason, Jason's mom did everything for him. "She took really good care of him," is Jodie's kind assessment of the situation. His family and friends all gave her the same warning—"Brace yourself. He's not going to be much help around the house."

While they were dating, Jodie and Jason talked about her concerns. She highly recommends a workbook entitled *Preparing for Marriage*.[1] The workbook is comprised of various topics, including expectations regarding housework. They shared their opinions on how things should be done, discussed "his and her" jobs, and considered how they could work together to get everything accomplished.

Looking back, Jodie reflects, "It was awesome. Jason is a wonderful helpmate. I do certain jobs, he does others, and we do some things together."

Fifty/Fifty?

My story is slightly different. I do certain jobs, I do others, and the rest of the jobs, I do. We hadn't heard of any such workbook back when we were dating. At this point in our relationship, I think it's a bit late to pick one up.

As newlyweds, Gabe and I divided our responsibilities around the house about 90/10. And I'm being generous in my estimate. For the most part, I accepted the heavier load without issue. Occasionally, I would let bitterness creep in—especially when I started teaching full-time. Gabe was still in school, and I was shouldering a full workload and all of the housekeeping duties. (I know, I already admitted that I never cleaned. Oops.)

I have friends whose husbands do the laundry or clean the bathrooms or run the vacuum. Gabe is not one of those men. And that's okay. I really don't mind. (In all fairness, he does take out the trash, fix things around the house, and play with our girls.) Each couple is different, basing their division of household tasks on different factors.

First of all, we all come into marriage with preconceived ideas. Did his dad do dishes, or did his mom? Who cleaned the bathroom? Who vacuumed? Who took out the trash? This often determines how we think things should be.

We also have to take into account each other's responsibilities outside the home. Does your hubby work ten hours a day while you work five? Are you the breadwinner while your husband goes to school? Some couples deal with illnesses or physical limitations, and the healthy partner carries the heavier load by default.

There's no right or wrong way to divide up the chores, but you and your husband need to reach some sort of agreement, or things will be rough.

Karol Ladd shares some great insights in her book *The Power of a*

Positive Wife. She says that even when you compromise, the break-down of the household tasks may not seem completely fair. "Be willing to take on more than your fair share," she says. "Here's why: no spouse sees the entire weight of the workload that the other spouse carries during the day. If you're going to err, err on the side of giving, not getting."[2]

Doesn't that fly in the face of what we consider to be our basic rights? None of us likes the idea of doing more than our fair share!

One woman told me, "Before I was married, I thought it would be 50/50, with both people helping around the house."

We love to talk about 50/50 as if it's some objective goal that can actually be reached. But who gets to assign point values to individual household chores? "Even" distribution is highly subjective. You and hubby are not likely to agree on the rules.

My feelings? Do your part faithfully, regardless of whether or not your husband upholds his end of the bargain. If you begin to feel resentful, pray that God will calm you with His peace. If you feel the need to confront your husband, do it only after spending time in prayer. Don't waste time nagging—men rarely respond well to it.

All She's Cracked Up to Be?

I know some of you still aren't sold on the idea of this Proverbs 31 chick. You love your husband, you love the Lord, but you just can't imagine accepting such an old-fashioned way of looking at your home and marriage.

"This is the twenty-first century!" you want to shout across these pages into my face. "She just isn't *relevant* anymore!" I see your point. I really do.

I came across a blog last week, and the phrase "Proverbs 31 woman" caught my eye. The writer's main point was that if she had servant girls like the woman in Proverbs 31, she too would be able to accomplish the lengthy list of tasks laid out in those 22 jam-packed verses.

She commented that Christian women spend too much time comparing themselves to her and then feeling inadequate when they don't measure up. She was determined not to waste valuable time and energy comparing herself to "Mrs. P31."

She admitted that the chapter has lots of valuable little "gems worth taking to heart" but maintains that we shouldn't use it as a checklist as I jokingly did earlier in this chapter. Rose at dawn? Check. Supplied the merchants with sashes? Check.

"It's not a magic formula," she commented. "After all, if I had servants and didn't have to scrub my toilets and floors, I'd be out buying vineyards too. Wouldn't you?"

Another woman pointed out that the P31 gal was persnickety about her clothing, was always leaving her children to work away from home, and delegated most of her chores to others. So in light of all that, what are we supposed to think of her?

What I Think

I don't believe God would have given this woman her own page in the Bible if He didn't want us to learn something from her. He knows we aren't capable of living up to her seeming perfection. But as a perfect, holy God, He can't lower His standards.

So far today, have you gossiped, lied, said something unkind, been impatient, lost your temper, envied someone, been discontent, failed to trust God to provide, botched a chance to share Christ with a coworker, watched a TV show with questionable content, eaten too much, or been prideful?

"You know," muses God, "I'm asking too much of them. Let's get rid of a couple of those really tough ones. How about being patient?

What about gossiping? I can't expect My children to always be patient and to never gossip, can I?"

Just because we can't get through a day without messing up doesn't mean God starts taking commands out of the Bible.

Thankfully, Proverbs 31 isn't written as a list of commandments. "Thou shalt rise when it is still dark and sew all your own clothing," and so on. We are simply given an example of a woman who was worthy of praise, and we are to emulate her as best we can. She is the highest standard, something to shoot for.

Times have changed, yes, but basic principles have not. Loving your husband and caring for your family are still vitally important. How you do those things may be different from the way women did them thousands of years ago, and you may do them differently than your neighbor does, but they're still important.

We can look past the fine linen and the distaff, the merchant ships and the city gate, the vineyard and the flax, and find valuable truths that can guide us and inspire us to be women and wives after God's own heart.

If the Bible had been written in the year 2006, Mrs. P31 might be doing all her trading online and selling her goods on eBay. Sewing her linens on a Euro Pro 9105 computerized sewing machine (or buying them on sale at Target) and working out at the YMCA. The specifics of her daily life would have changed, but I guarantee you that her values and work ethics would not.

Read between the lines and find the valuable gems that are both timely and timeless. Noble character...full confidence in her...lacks nothing of value...brings him good, not harm...works with eager hands...works vigorously...profitable...opens her arms...no fear... her husband is respected...strength and dignity...wisdom...faithful instruction...children call her blessed...husband praises her...fears the Lord.

I'm standing up in defense of the Proverbs 31 woman. I want to be like her. Not a fabulous seamstress or a planter of vineyards, but like her in character. I want to be praised not for my beauty or my charm or anything else temporal, but because I fear the Lord. When I go home to meet my Savior, I want Him to say to me, "Well done, good and faithful servant!" Are you with me?

Getting Practical

My aunt Dawn lives hundreds of miles away and visited my home for the first time this summer. We took a quick tour of my house, starting with my kitchen.

"So tell me, Marla, are you domestic?" she wanted to know, as she looked around.

"Well, it depends on what you mean by 'domestic,'" I said.

"You know, do you like to cook and bake and all that?"

"Well, I do like to cook. And I bake chocolate chip cookies every once in a while. Does that make me domestic?"

She said it did.

How domestic is domestic enough? Is there anything inherently wrong with a Christian woman *not* being domestic? Is it something we're born with? Do we have to work at developing it? Does it even matter? If I want to be a good wife and homemaker, what do I need to do exactly? Give me a checklist.

There is no simple answer. Every woman's situation is different. Your background, education, personality, skills and talents, current job, and husband will all play a role in your homemaking.

I've read books by godly women who wouldn't dream of serving their husbands a meal on a paper plate or making them eat a frozen burrito (microwaved, of course!). I'm not one of those women.

I do like to cook, and I try to make a variety of tasty meals, but that can be costly and time-consuming. Sometimes I'm short on funds, and grilled cheese sandwiches are a cost-effective choice. Other times, the money is there but not the time. Chinese takeout!

Pray for wisdom, and do what God tells you is best for you and your husband.

To Cook or Not to Cook

If you have an embarrassing cooking, baking, or kitchen story from your early days of marriage, join the club! When I asked my survey takers to share humorous stories from the beginning stages of wedded wifehood, culinary mishaps were the theme of the hour.

Burnt cookies, homemade bread the consistency of a jawbreaker, glass casserole dishes breaking in the oven with their contents oozing all over creation, "hot" meals that were served still frozen in the center…

Gabe's aunt Chris told me about the first morning she ever cooked breakfast for her new husband. "I went to put potatoes in a pan of grease to fry and had the control on high," she says. "The grease went flying all over and sizzled my hair and Jim's. We ate cereal from then on." Thirty-two years later, Uncle Jim has hardly any hair. I always wondered why…

My friend Pat comments that "cooking was not my forte when we were first married." She remembers being thankful that her husband, Rick, was a Marine. "After being out on the field and eating the canned and packaged meals, anything I made tasted good to him, except for our first Thanksgiving…"

She went on to relate a story of cold, lumpy potatoes, burnt corn, and an incompletely cooked turkey with the completely melted plastic bag of giblets she failed to remove from the neck cavity. Rick was gracious throughout the entire meal and snacked on popcorn when he got hungry again soon afterward.

My friend Wendy bought a frozen pumpkin pie for her and Dan's first Thanksgiving dinner. She took it out of the freezer and drove to her in-laws. Her plan was to let the pie thaw out on the trip there so they could eat it after dinner.

"I didn't know I had to bake it!" she bemoans. "It spilled all over my seat!"

My sister-in-law Angie laughs at her own lack of culinary expertise when she and Tug were first married. "How do you burn macaroni and cheese *and* set off the smoke alarm?" she asks. "Does that mean I'm a bad cook?" In the years since, I've sampled plenty of tasty dishes she's prepared. If you want to learn to cook, there's nothing stopping you. Just remember to give yourself time—practice makes perfect!

A Haven-ly Home

A big part of bringing your husband good, not harm, all the days of his life is making your home a haven for him—and for you. It should be warm and inviting, clean and uncluttered.

Our homes are important—our own little corners of the world where we can kick back and relax, rest, and recharge. Our homes should be places our husbands long to return to—not somewhere they want to escape from. And deep down inside us, I think we long to be queen of a home where our husband is king.

Sit down in an easy chair in your home and take a look around. Does it feel calm and relaxing or crazy and chaotic? Do you have to move a pile or two to even find a place to sit? Here are a few simple steps to take if your home is less than a haven.

1. *Have a place for everything, and put everything in its place.* Giving everything a home makes returning something so much easier when you're done with it. You'll save loads of time in the long run.

2. *Keep up with chores.* Anytime you get too far behind on dishes or laundry or whatever, it gets easier to let it keep sliding. As soon as you get a basketful of dirty clothes, wash them. Rinse your dishes off

as you use them, load them immediately in the dishwasher (if you have one), and never let them get piled up too high.

3. *Waste not, want not.* Be a good steward. Don't let food rot because you didn't eat it. Don't buy in bulk if you can't consume it fast enough or if you will tire of it before it's gone.

4. *Pray that God will help you use your time and money wisely.* Should you order pizza so you can use that hour of cooking time to pursue something more valuable? Or should you cook a cheap meal and use the ten dollars you saved for God's glory in another way?

5. *Simplify, simplify, simplify.* Get rid of junk you don't need. Get out of the habit of buying things you'll never use just because they were on sale. Maintaining stuff is stressful and time-consuming. I finally have this one almost mastered. It feels good.

The Art of Hospitality

One last thing about your home—share it with others. The Bible talks about opening up your home, practicing hospitality, and giving others a good meal and a place to stay. It even says that some of us, by sharing our home with strangers, may have entertained angels without knowing it (Hebrews 13:2).

In Romans 15, Paul writes to the church in Rome about his plans to visit them soon. He has a few stopovers—a couple of unpleasant tasks to handle—before he can finally relax with them.

"Then, God willing, I'll be on my way to you with a light and eager heart, looking forward to being refreshed by your company" (verse 32 MSG). The very thought of their visit is going to help him get through his difficult journey.

"My hope is that my visit with you is going to be one of Christ's more extravagant blessings," he says (verse 29 MSG). What if we prayed that verse before we had guests in our home? "Lord, help us to bless our guests extravagantly during this visit."

Toben and Joanne Heim say, "We feel strongly that our house is really God's house, and we want Him to use it however He chooses."[3]

Opening your home to others is hard if it's a wreck. My goal is to keep my house looking good at all times so that if guests drop by unannounced, I won't be embarrassed to invite them in. I want them to feel welcome and comfortable, not sidestepping piles of messes.

"Our apartment is too tiny," I used to say. "When I have a house, I'll invite people over." Well, now I have a house and no excuse. I still have to exert myself to call friends up and ask them to come for a meal or a visit. But I feel so much better once I do.

Toben Heim agrees. "It seems like Joanne and I always get along best when we are inviting people into our home or getting out of the house to help others."[4]

The Heart of the Matter

Feminist or traditionalist, career minded or domestic, as a woman, you are the heart of your dwelling place. Most men don't have the knack we do for making a house feel like a home. If you want a warm and inviting living environment, it's up to you.

As women, we have opportunities to honor God in many different spheres of influence. Regardless of your job, career, or position in the outside world, living for the Lord starts in your own home. Ask God what changes you need to make in this area today.

Where Is Your Treasure?

Do not store up for yourselves treasures on earth…
but store up for yourselves treasures in heaven…
for where your treasure is, there your heart will be also.

MATTHEW 6:19-21

"By the time I pay my bills, my paycheck's almost gone!" I lamented to my dad a week before my wedding day. "I don't have any money left for anything *fun!*"

Expecting heartfelt sympathy, I got hearty laughter instead.

"Welcome to the real world, dear," he said. "This is what being an adult is all about." Not what I wanted to hear.

Don't be fooled. Money is a big issue in marriage. That may be hard to imagine while you're dating. Many of us lived at home until we got married or lived in a college dorm. We didn't have any living expenses—just new clothes and toys, eating out and entertainment. Marriage is a whole new ball game.

I think my first clue came six months after I graduated from college and had to pay the first installment on my school loan. My life as I knew it—from a financial standpoint anyway—was over. Then I got married…

Bills, Bills, Bills

At first glance, the financial aspect of marriage was new and exciting. I remember the first time I saw checks with both our names on them. I felt so grown-up! Even our first bill was a treat!

"Our very first real married-people bill!" I remember thinking with a smile.

Yeah, well…the smiles stopped there. In only a matter of weeks, the bills started flooding in faster than our tiny little paychecks could carry them. Just checking the mailbox was enough to send me into a temporary depression.

For the first few months of our marriage, Gabe was working part-time and going to school full-time. I was subbing part-time. And we had a truckload of bills.

The worst were my school bills. Thankfully, Gabe's wouldn't come due for two more years. The thought of putting four days of subbing earnings toward my school bill each month was disheartening.

"Why in the world did I go to a Christian college?" I moaned. "I'll have to work the rest of my life just to pay back my loans!"

I was beginning to think that Cedarville University's motto came straight from Proverbs 4:7—"Though it cost all you have, get understanding."

I felt compelled to rewrite that verse as a warning to prospective students. "College will cost all you have! And then drive you even further into debt! You'll rue the day you borrowed money in the name of higher education! Is it *really* that necessary to get knowledge and understanding? I don't think so!" (Proverbs 4:7, Marla's Amplified Version).

One thing's for sure. I had more empathy for my parents. My dad worked hard his whole life to faithfully bring home a paycheck each week, and what happened to it? It was gobbled up by bills and devoured by us four kids.

Gabe and I couldn't do much to reduce the amount we owed each month for rent, school, and utilities. But we did have a cost-effective plan for our phone bill.

Anytime we needed to talk to dear ol' Mom or Dad, we'd dial them up, and say sweetly, "Could you call me back?" Pretty soon, we had them so well trained that as soon as they heard one of our voices— click! Then, *brrrrrring!* What moochers! We have since learned to shoulder more responsibility.

I remember a month when we made 40 long-distance phone calls for less than five dollars. Just the year before, as I called Gabe from Japan, our phone calls often cost five times that much *apiece!* Our phone bill was the only bill to go *down* after we got married.

So Much to Say

Money plays a big role in marriage. Remember that study that asked couples what they fought about most—his mother, her mother, sex, and…money! Just like sex, household finance is the topic of entire books. I obviously can't cover everything here, so I'll pick and choose what I feel will be most helpful.

In this chapter, you won't get specifics on how to balance a check-book, draw up a workable budget, or save for the future—even though I *will* share a few practical tips that have made a difference in my marriage.

What you will find, however, are truths from God's Word about money, what Jesus Himself had to say on the topic, and how your heart and your money are intricately intertwined.

Jesus spoke more on the subject of money than on heaven and hell combined. If He spent that much of His three-year earthly ministry talking about it, it must be important. Jesus didn't waste words!

In this chapter, I want us to reconsider how we view money. I want us to see it through God's eyes and discover His plan for our financial resources. How God calls you to spend your money will be different from how He calls me to spend mine. The important thing is that we listen to God's voice in every aspect of life—including our finances.

"Only when we recognize that all we have comes from God," Stormie Omartian says, "and seek to make Him Lord over it can we avoid the pitfalls that money, or the lack of it, brings. So many money problems can be solved by putting all finances under God's covering and doing what He says to do with them."[1]

So, how do we look at money God's way?

God's Word on Money

I've gleaned two important concepts from the money verses in the Bible—don't love money, and be content with what you have.

The love of money is a root of all kinds of evil, the Bible says. You would think it would be something else. Money seems fairly harmless.

But God knows that our love of money is the motivating factor behind nearly everything we do that is displeasing to Him. So many of us Christians claim to have surrendered everything to Christ—all but our checkbooks, that is. Money grips us more tightly than does anything else on earth. If we're going to be truly happy in life, we have to give our money to God.

One of my all-time favorite quotes reads, "Contentment is not the fulfillment of what you want but the realization of how much you already have."

If you haven't learned to be content with what you have, if your heart is not in the right place concerning money, no amount of budgeting or strategizing will cure your financial woes.

"Whoever loves money never has money enough," we're told in Ecclesiastes 5:10 (by the richest man in the world, no less). "Whoever loves wealth is never satisfied with his income."

Hebrews 13:5 tells us to "keep your lives free from the love of money and be content with what you have, because God has said, 'Never will I leave you; never will I forsake you.'"

The psalmist warns us, "Though your riches increase, do not set your heart on them" (63:10). And Solomon says that wealth will "sprout wings and fly off" (Proverbs 23:5).

If you want to know more about what God has to say on the topic of money, do yourself a huge favor and read Randy Alcorn's *Money, Possessions, and Eternity* and *The Treasure Principle*. Alcorn has done extensive research on God's thoughts concerning our finances. These books will revolutionize the way you view your money—and your life.

Giving God His Due

How much money you give to God is between you and Him. Once you're married, your husband enters the equation. I do believe that we should follow the biblical example of giving at least one tenth of all we earn back to the Lord.

I also believe we should tithe from our gross income, not the amount we see in our paychecks. If we are to give our "first fruits" to God, we should let God have His cut before Uncle Sam snatches his.

Someone once told Randy Alcorn he couldn't possibly afford to give God 10 percent of his income. Randy asked him if he would *die* if he were forced to live off just 90 percent of his wages.

"Well no, of course not," the man replied.

"Then you can afford to tithe," Randy told him.

When money has been painfully tight and we've been tempted not to tithe, God has rewarded our obedience. And when we've upped our giving to more than 10 percent at times when money still wasn't plentiful, He has blessed us. Money has come out of nowhere to pay our bills.

One question people have asked me—and I have asked of others—

is "Do I have to give my whole tithe to the church, or can I give to other Christian organizations?"

I'm not going to tell you what to do. Pray about it. Ask God for wisdom. Study Bible passages on giving, and ask God to show you what He means by them.

As a general rule, we have given 10 percent to our church, and any additional giving came out of the remaining 90 percent. At times, though, we have used a month's tithe to send Christmas boxes to children in third-world countries or to support missionaries.

Just remember—your church depends on your financial support. If half the church stopped giving money and gave it elsewhere, the church could not survive.

What about tithing to places like the Red Cross or the American Cancer Society? Those are wonderful causes, and you are free to give money to them if you choose. But they are not dedicated to sharing the gospel with the people they help—and our tithe is to belong to *God*.

Evaluate your spending at all times. When you buy things you don't need or let things go to waste, you've thrown away money that you could have used for God's glory. Being responsible with the money we've been given means more freedom to give to people in need. God expects good stewardship out of His children. Someday, I believe, we'll all be held accountable for every dollar that has ever passed through our fingers.

Money Rewards

We shouldn't give money away just so God will give it back to us in some form. But I've found that when I do the right thing with my money, God *always* rewards me—often monetarily.

One instance that stands out in my mind happened during my freshman year at college. My friend Sarah and I were walking out of the dining hall, and we spotted a twenty-dollar bill lying on the floor. No one was around but us.

Sarah picked it up and turned to me. "What should we do with it?" she asked.

We silently weighed our options. Keep it or turn it in. We could each have ten dollars of free spending money, or we could walk down to the admissions office and hand it over in case some needy student came looking for his lost twenty-dollar bill.

We looked at each other, sighed, and headed for the office.

Later, as we walked to the post office on that chilly fall day, I felt a sense of loss. That ten dollars would have been nice. But I also felt a sense of peace, knowing we had done the right thing.

As I opened my post office box, a letter from my grandma and grandpa fell out. I smiled and opened the envelope. It was a Happy Thanksgiving card. I opened the card and gasped. Tucked inside was a crisp twenty-dollar bill. I looked up, half expecting to see an angel in the sky or even God Himself smiling down on me.

What makes this even more unusual is that my grandparents have 26 grandkids plus their spouses—and not a lot of money. Growing up, we would get two dollars for our birthdays and ten dollars for Christmas. Never twenty dollars—and never on any other holidays. I haven't gotten that much money—or any money on Thanksgiving—from them since. To this day, Grandma doesn't remember sending me twenty dollars. Thanks, God!

Sometimes I've written a check to our church in faith, wondering where the money would come from to buy groceries for the coming week. We've gotten unexpected refunds from the phone company, insurance companies, even the government.

Whatever you do, don't be tempted to cut back on your giving to God when you find yourselves deep in debt. Tithing is important, and you will find that when you trust God with your first 10 percent, He will miraculously provide for you in other areas.

Money Troubles in Marriage

If you and your husband ever fight about money, you're not alone. In fact, more than 50 percent of all couples who get divorced cite financial disputes as the primary factor in their split. Scary thought!

I asked some women to share with me some problems that money has caused in their marriages, hoping for some insight to share with you. I wasn't disappointed.

My friend Mary Ann told me that money was at the root of one of her earliest married fights. "I bought something Dan thought I didn't need," she recalls, "and we couldn't afford."

"Early on, we fought about money," one woman said. "Especially when he left to do something that required money, and I had to stay home!"

This is a good one. How do you like your husband spending money on things that don't involve you? Makes you want to go on a little shopping spree, doesn't it?

One friend told me that household finance was the biggest stumbling block early on in their marriage. "We took a little while to get on the same wavelength," she says.

This is probably an understatement—a nice way of saying, "We went through hell on earth trying to make sense of our different perspectives on money."

One woman went with her husband to a budgeting workshop after their struggles with spending, saving, and giving got a bit overwhelming. She says the input really helped.

My sister Bethany found out that she and her husband also had some different ideas—she prefers quality, and Stewart is all about quantity.

"I'd rather get fewer nice things," she says. "Stewart splurges on junk food and the dollar store but gives me a hard time for spending extra money on groceries or name brand toothbrushes."

They're learning the difference between things they want and things they need. And finding good deals and sharing those finds has become a bonding time for them.

Other differences were the result of different backgrounds. "Financially, he had no limits growing up," one woman told me. "I did."

"My family had money but didn't spend anything," said another. "His family didn't have money but enjoyed it."

"He was raised in a well-off, two-parent home," my friend Hailey told me. "My mom was a single mother just getting by. It's taken a lot of discussions and compromises to deal with how to handle finances."

One woman was basing her ideas about money on her childhood and found the philosophy didn't transfer well to her marriage.

"I have an older brother," she says, "and always felt that things should be evenly distributed. That doesn't work in marriage. Neither does keeping a record of money spent by each other to keep things even!"

One friend told me that she and her husband were polar opposites when it came to money. She was stingy, and he bought everything on a whim. After many years, they've learned to compromise and find a happy medium.

When you say "I do," you're not just beginning a marriage, you're starting a business! But it's so much more than that. Money matters are heart matters. Fights about money are never just about money. They're about power and control, self-worth and insecurity, selfishness and stubbornness.

If you're dealing with money problems in your marriage, ask God to reveal to you the deeper issues at the heart of it all.

Emotional Spending

How does spending money make you feel? Is it therapeutic? Soothing? Emotionally gratifying? Buying things just makes me feel good. My husband hurts my feelings. I buy something. Rough day at work. I buy something. It's Friday night, and I survived the week. I need to buy something.

For many women, spending is an emotional thing, much like eating. Show me a woman addicted to shopping, and I'll show you a woman who is hurting, lacking, or angry.

The problem with spending money to fill a hole in our lives is that it simply doesn't work. In many cases, our spending habits make the hole even bigger.

When I buy something to comfort myself, that warm, fuzzy feeling usually lasts just long enough for me to get my purchase home and out of the bag. And then I think of something else I "need."

Are you someone who has closets and boxes full of clothes and merchandise with all the price tags still secured? Why do you feel the need to accumulate so much stuff? To feel good about yourself? Is it working?

We are warned in Luke 12:15 to "Watch out! Be on your guard against all kinds of greed; a man's life does not consist in the abundance of his possessions."

Do you define yourself by your stuff?

Jesus tells a story in the ensuing verses in Luke 12 about a man who stored up much for himself. He had so much stuff, he made plans to build bigger and better storage units to hold it all. God wasn't pleased with his selfishness and took the man's life that very night.

"This is how it will be," Jesus warned, "with anyone who stores up things for himself but is not rich toward God" (verse 21).

Debilitating Debt

What about debt? Debt comes in two flavors—acceptable debt and unacceptable debt.

Debt of the acceptable variety includes a home mortgage, school loans, and possibly a car loan.

Unacceptable debt comes from using a credit card to buy something you do not need and cannot pay for when the monthly statement comes due. Items in this category include (but are not limited to) clothing, furniture, a new deck in your backyard, eating out, a cappuccino on the way to work, and so on and so forth.

My husband and I currently have $3000 in credit card debt. Not too long ago, it was nearly three times that amount. My prayer is that once this book gets published, we'll pay off the last of our credit cards. Forever.

Over the six-year course of our marriage, we've been in and out and in and out and in and out of debt. I brought school loans into our marriage, and Gabe's started just a couple years later. We were fortunate to not have a car payment until year five of our marriage, but we've had one for the last two years.

I've taught school full-time, subbed, worked at a nursing home, done freelance writing, and been a full-time mom since I've been married.

Gabe has been a full-time student and a pizza delivery boy, worked at an Internet company as tech support, had four corporate jobs, worked at a church camp, and now is self-employed.

We have made so many moves and transitions it's not funny. We've lived eleven different places in seven years of marriage. Each time we've relocated, our lives have been turned upside down for a time, and all our money has come flying out of our pockets. Getting everything back in order financially hasn't been fun.

We have been poor, rich, poor, kind of poor, well-off, really poor, pretty well-off, poor...you get the picture. We've seen it all. Three times.

I want to share something with you from personal experience. One small financial tip that I want you to take very seriously. It will save you a lifetime of grief.

Do...not...rack...up...one...cent...of...credit...card...debt.

Credit card debt is debilitating, depressing, disparaging, deceptive, dangerous, deploring, detrimental, disabling, disastrous, discomforting, discouraging, disgraceful, dismal, disheartening, and divisive.

The bottom line is this: Credit cards have ruined many a marriage. The only way to be sure it doesn't happen to you is to never put more on a credit card than you can pay off within that month. Or my personal favorite—just don't use them at all. You can use a check card instead. Then the money comes directly out of your account.

When you save your money and pay cash up front for a purchase, you appreciate the item infinitely more than if you charge it on impulse. God created us to work and be rewarded for that work. He created us to find satisfaction in the work of our hands, not in our signature on a credit card slip.

As Calvin Coolidge once said, "There is no dignity quite so impressive, and no independence quite so important, as living within your means." I couldn't agree more. We've gone nine months now without putting a single purchase on a credit card, and boy, does it feel good.

Getting Out of Debt

Most of us have made financial blunders of one sort or another in the past—and probably in the present as well. I know I've made more than my fair share.

Put the past behind you and determine to start anew today. It won't be easy, but you need to do it. Don't give in to the temptation to say, "I've already screwed up so badly I might as well keep on spending. What's another $50 on a $10,000 credit card bill?"

You have to start somewhere! Start today!

I cannot tell you how to get out of debt without knowing how much debt you have and how you came to be in such a deep hole. I can, however, give you some general guidelines.

The key to paying back credit card debt is to *never rack up any new debt.* In order to do this, you may not be able to pay back as much each month as you'd like. If you have an extra hundred dollars, you may be tempted to put it all toward the credit card. But then what happens when you run out of money and need gas? It goes on the credit card. Better to put $50 toward the card and save $50 for emergencies.

Try to save a little money while you're paying off your credit card. Ideally, you could pay off your credit card quick as lightning and then start saving, but that probably isn't going to happen. Keep some money set aside to use if you absolutely have to—to avoid adding any more debt to your cards.

You also need to set a budget—one you can genuinely live with. Just as ultra-strict diets never last long, neither do ultra-strict budgets. If you don't budget in at least a small amount for movie rentals, a date night or two, and something little (but fun) you want to buy, you're asking for trouble.

If you budget only $100 for groceries for the entire month and use it all after ten days, you're just going to run out to the store and put $100 of your favorite foods on your credit card. Aren't you?

Try putting cash into different envelopes at the beginning of each month. Each envelope is designated for a certain expense—tithing, groceries, gas, eating out, toiletries, medical expenses, and the like. When the money is gone for the month, you're out of luck!

If you still need gas and your gas envelope is empty, you might have to eat grilled cheese sandwiches at home one Friday night and use some of your eating out money to put gas in your car.

Sitting down together and working out a budget can be a great way to agree on your spending and saving habits as well as your financial expectations.

One thing to remember is that regardless of how you got into debt, God is more than willing to help pull you out. Humble yourself before Him and ask Him to help you.

Saving for a Rainy Day

I am in no position to be telling you to save your money. I haven't had money in my savings account since I was ten. I have plans to start saving really soon though…

Many people believe you should save or invest at least 10 percent of your income. Sounds like a good idea to me. If you don't do it systematically though—like through direct deposit—you probably won't have the discipline to do it.

Some people think saving money means buying things on sale. "I just bought a $100 jacket (that I don't need) on sale for $15! I saved $85!"

Um…no, you didn't actually *save* anything. You *spent* $15. There's a big difference. Saving money means *not spending* it.

One fun way to save money is to go to the grocery store with a certain amount of cash in your pocket. Be as careful as you can, finding good deals and ways to stretch your money. Your goal is to get to the checkout counter, pay for your groceries, and have money left over. The money you didn't spend can go directly into your savings account.

By the way, I highly recommend using cash anytime you go shopping—whether it's for groceries, clothing, or whatever. Researchers have proven that with a card in your hand, you will probably spend up to 30 percent more than you would if you carried cash.

Having some money set aside is important. When we don't have any savings, and something suddenly comes up—emergency surgery, blown transmission, broken pipes—we have no choice but to put it on our credit card.

And the vicious cycle continues.

Money Isn't Everything

One thing that stands out in my mind about my favorite child-hood memories (and my memories of dating Gabe) is that most of them were simple and cost little money or none at all.

Somehow, we've gotten the idea that having fun means spending money. Nice restaurants, movie theaters, shopping malls, amusement parks—they all want our money in exchange for a good time.

But when we get right down to it, the most memorable times in our lives were times when we made do with what we had, when we were content with what we'd been given.

In Paul's first letter to Timothy, he tells him that "godliness with contentment is great gain. For we brought nothing into this world, and we can take nothing out of it. But if we have food and clothing, we will be content with that" (1 Timothy 6:6-8).

Couples with little or no money can have just as much fun as those who have been financially blessed—and sometimes even more!

Start early in your marriage celebrating days that God did something special for you—a new job, a raise, a good grade, even a really good day. You can celebrate the anniversary of the day you met, your first date, the day you got engaged. You can even celebrate "I love you" days.

You don't have to live by the calendar. You know, all those holidays written in tiny print at the bottom of the calendar squares. Those are all great occasions to celebrate. But you can also add a few special ones of your own.

Depending on your situation, you might feel as if you don't have a whole lot to get excited about. If you're struggling financially, trying to get through college, looking for jobs, you might not think you have cause—or the funds—to celebrate.

But celebrating doesn't have to be expensive or elaborate. Get creative. Learn not only to be content with what you've got but to use your limited resources to live life richly and abundantly.

An Attitude of Gratitude

I often get so caught up in the "I needs" that I forget to cultivate a spirit of thankfulness in my heart for the "I already haves." Keeping track of the blessings and provisions God sends my way—and taking the time to thank Him for them—goes a long way in fostering an attitude of gratitude in my life. And God's provisions aren't always financial.

I remember one morning in particular just months after our wedding. I was a mess. My alarm clock had malfunctioned, and I was rushing around like a headless chicken. I had a subbing job to get to, and I was late.

Gabe stood and watched it all with a smile on his face. "You gonna be all right?" he asked as he kissed me goodbye.

"Of course," I said, not convincing either one of us.

"You look nice," he offered, trying to help.

"Hmm," I mumbled as I flew out the door. I had managed to put myself together fairly well, but I had forgotten one very important detail.

I realized it about half an hour later as I sat in the teacher's chair, waiting for the students to arrive. I leafed through her lesson plans, hoping for an easy day, and suddenly gasped out loud. I had forgotten to put deodorant on that morning—I just knew it—and being in new and unpredictable situations always made me sweat. I lifted up my arm and took a sniff. Sure enough, no powder-fresh scent, just the beginning traces of body odor.

What was I going to do? Just the thought of my missing antiperspirant made me start to drip. "Lord, help me," I prayed. I even thought about calling Gabe and asking him to bring me some deodorant. But he had already left for work.

Then I remembered a can of air freshener I had seen in the staff restroom just 15 minutes before. It turned out to be a divine revelation. I knew air freshener had no antiperspirant in it (why would it?), but maybe if I sprayed some on my armpits, it would disguise the odor for at least a little while. I didn't happen to notice what scent it was—preferably Fresh Linen and not Cinnamon.

I now had roughly two minutes before the students were scheduled to arrive. I rushed to the restroom. There was the air freshener atop the paper towel dispenser. I grabbed it and sprayed one pit and then the other, praying it wouldn't burn. As I lowered the can, my jaw dropped. The air freshener was not air freshener at all. It was a can of antiperspirant and deodorant—powder-fresh scent and all! It was all I could do not to shout praises out loud to God down the hallway!

After lunch, I visited the restroom again. When I walked in the door, lo and behold, the deodorant was gone. God had put it there just for me!

Do you ever find yourself overlooking God's little provisions? Have you thanked Him lately for the roof over your head, the food on your table, and the clothes on your back? How about the fresh, juicy strawberries on sale at the grocery, the generous compliment from your boss, or the letter in the mail from a long-lost friend? Or the extra-sunny day, the nest of birds outside your window, or the smell of freshly cut grass? Have you thanked Him for your husband? God is good!

Giving It to God

I still get a bit worked up at times over bills and money. And I have to ask God to help me to focus on all the blessings of life and marriage and not the burdens. Besides, if I were financially set, if money were no object, I would miss out on the joy of trusting in the Lord.

He has always come through for Gabe and me financially (and in every other way). I can't ask for anything more.

Are finances a burden to you? Are you letting the bills and loans and debts get you down? How about handing them over to your heavenly Father and letting *Him* worry about them?

Matthew 6:25-34 tells us not to worry about what we'll eat or drink or wear. If God can take care of the birds and flowers, of course He'll take care of us. We can't add a single hour to our lives by worrying.

Think of some of the financial burdens you've been carrying, and pray that God will help you to trust completely in Him for your every need. Your prayer might go something like this:

> Father, thank You for promising to meet my every need according to Your glorious riches in Christ Jesus (Philippians 4:19).
>
> Thank You, seriously, for our financial struggles. As Paul said so eloquently, things happen to us "that we might not rely on ourselves but on God" (2 Corinthians 1:9).
>
> Thank You for giving me only what I need for today and showing me that if I had more than enough, I might think I didn't need You (Proverbs 30:8-9).

Help us to appreciate all we've been given and to joyfully trust You. Help us to focus on what we have, not on what we don't. Thank You for being a God and Savior who daily bears our burdens.

The Final Word

Listen to advice and accept instruction,
and in the end you will be wise.

When I got engaged, everyone and her sister had advice for me—"helpful" tips on wedding plans, honeymoon locations, getting along with my new husband. I just smiled and nodded, ignoring most of it.

Two weeks before the wedding, I was subbing for a great group of fourth graders. We had done everything on the teacher's list and still had time left in the day. On impulse, I passed out slips of paper and asked them for advice about my upcoming wedding and marriage. There was no end to their helpful suggestions.

> "If someone else asks you to get married, go ahead and marry the first person. Don't cancel your marriage or you might regret it."

> "Smile at your fiancé and brush your teeth and take a breath mint."

> "Don't get married if that boy is ugly."

> "Be wise about your husbands and try not to make the wrong choices."

> "Don't marry someone stupid."

"Don't make it like on *America's Funniest Wedding Mess-Ups*."

"Don't marry a slime ball."

"Stop the marriage and marry me!"

That last one was my personal favorite. At the end of the day little Ryan, the author of those words, approached me shyly and said, "You know when they tie those cans to the back of your car?"

"Yeah?" I said.

"Well, I'll be hanging on tight to one of those!"

You've got to love flattery.

In all seriousness, advice is great, but before we act on it or even accept it as truth, we need to not only consider the source (nine-year-olds in this case) but also consult the one true Source to see if that advice lines up with His Word.

Hopefully, by this point you feel that you know me to some degree, that you can trust me, that I have experience from which to share, and that I'm committed to living by the principles in God's Word. But remember—don't take me at my word without checking what I say against Scripture.

I have a much better grasp of God's plan for marriage and my role as a wife than I did when I first got married. I'm learning how to be more selfless and put what I've learned into practice far more often than I once did. I'm learning how to pray for Gabe and how to wait patiently for God to work. I'm learning how to put off self-pity and put on grace and humility and forgiveness.

I still have so far to go! I'm definitely a work in progress (ask Gabe!). No delusions of perfection here. But I'm encouraged by the steps I've taken in the right direction.

As I wrote this book, I prayed that God would use me as a link between His heart and yours. I hope you gleaned some helpful information to guide you through this wonderful, bumpy journey called marriage.

And once again, I ask that you hold my words up to the Word to make sure they are in line with what God has to say. God will hold me accountable for the words I write. My prayer is that He will be glorified through this entire book—every chapter, every paragraph, every word.

I've really enjoyed our time together, friend. Let's talk again soon!

Notes

Let's Chat

1. Rick Warren, *The Purpose-Driven Life* (Grand Rapids: Zondervan, 2002), 247.
2. Ibid., 292.

Chapter 1—Great Expectations

1. Gary Chapman, *The Five Love Languages* (Chicago: Northfield, 1992), 29-30.
2. Gary Thomas, *Sacred Marriage* (Grand Rapids: Zondervan, 2000), 14-15.
3. Ibid., 16.
4. Karen Scalf Linamen, *Pillow Talk* (Grand Rapids: Fleming H. Revell, 1996), 16.
5. Toben and Joanne Heim, *Happily Ever After* (Colorado Springs: NavPress, 2004), 13.

Chapter 2—The First Year

1. Kevin Leman, *Sheet Music* (Wheaton, IL: Tyndale House, 2003), 65.
2. Ibid.
3. Toben and Joanne Heim, *Happily Ever After* (Colorado Springs: NavPress, 2004), 174.
4. David Boehi, et. al., *Preparing for Marriage* (Ventura, CA: Regal Books, 1997).
5. Heim, 16-17.

Chapter 3—It's Not About Me

1. Gary Thomas, *Sacred Marriage* (Grand Rapids: Zondervan, 2000).
2. Stormie Omartian, *The Power of a Praying Woman* (Eugene, OR: Harvest House Publishers, 2002), 20.

3. Stormie Omartian, *The Power of a Praying Wife* (Eugene, OR: Harvest House Publishers, 1997), 26.

4. Ibid., 13.

5. Toben and Joanne Heim, *Happily Ever After* (Colorado Springs: NavPress, 2004), 215.

Chapter 4—Fighting Fairly

1. Toben and Joanne Heim, *Happily Ever After* (Colorado Springs: NavPress, 2004), 71-73.

2. Ibid., 72-74.

3. Ibid., 75.

Chapter 5—Submission...Seriously?

1. H. Dale Burke, *Different by Design* (Chicago: Moody Press, 2000), 86-87.

2. Stormie Omartian, *The Power of a Praying Woman* (Eugene, OR: Harvest House Publishers, 2002), 19.

3. Toben and Joanne Heim, *Happily Ever After* (Colorado Springs: NavPress, 2004), 207.

4. Stormie Omartian, *The Power of a Praying Wife* (Eugene, OR: Harvest House Publishers, 1997), 38.

Chapter 6—R-E-S-P-E-C-T

1. H. Dale Burke, *Different by Design* (Chicago: Moody Press, 2000), 93.

2. Gary Thomas, *Sacred Marriage* (Grand Rapids: Zondervan, 2000), 57.

3. Karol Ladd, *The Power of a Positive Wife* (West Monroe, LA: Howard, 2003), 108.

4. Burke, 94.

Chapter 7—Family Matters

1. Toben and Joanne Heim, *Happily Ever After* (Colorado Springs: NavPress, 2004), 150.

2. Ibid., 27.

3. Ibid., 25.

Chapter 9—The Marriage Bed

1. Karen Scalf Linamen, *Pillow Talk* (Grand Rapids: Fleming H. Revell, 1996), 54.

2. Toben and Joanne Heim, *Happily Ever After* (Colorado Springs: NavPress, 2004), 118.

3. Linamen, 30.

4. Kevin Leman, *Sheet Music* (Wheaton, IL: Tyndale House, 2003), 10.

Chapter 10—Faithfulness in Action

1 Karen Scalf Linamen, *Pillow Talk* (Grand Rapids: Fleming H. Revell, 1996), 170-71.

2. Jill Savage, *Is There Really Sex After Kids?* (Grand Rapids: Zondervan, 2003), 138.

3. Linamen, 177.

4. Tim Alan Gardner, *Sacred Sex* (Colorado Springs: Waterbrook Press, 2002), 205.

5. Tommy Nelson, *The Book of Romance* (Nashville: Nelson Books, 1998), 155.

6. Gary Thomas, *Sacred Marriage* (Grand Rapids: Zondervan, 2000), 36.

Chapter 11—That Woman from Proverbs 31

1. David Boehi, et al., *Preparing for Marriage* (Ventura, CA: Regal Books, 1997).

2. Karol Ladd, *The Power of a Positive Wife* (West Monroe, LA: Howard Publishing, 2003), 220-21.

3. Toben and Joanne Heim, *Happily Ever After* (Colorado Springs: NavPress, 2004), 155.

4. Ibid., 156.

Chapter 12—Where Is Your Treasure?

1. Stormie Omartian, *The Power of a Praying Wife* (Eugene, OR: Harvest House Publishers, 1997), 55-56.

Other Great Harvest House
Books You'll Enjoy

JUST MARRIED
Margaret Feinberg

Just Married engagingly walks twentysomethings through their first years of marriage and tackles one of the biggest challenges for newlyweds—establishing their relationships with God both as individuals and as a married couple.

MEN ARE LIKE WAFFLES, WOMEN ARE LIKE SPAGHETTI
Bill and Pam Farrel

Men keep life elements in separate boxes; women intertwine everything. Providing biblical insights, sound research, and humorous anecdotes, the Farrels explore gender differences and preferences and how they can strengthen relationships.

BECOMING THE WOMAN OF HIS DREAMS
Sharon Jaynes

Becoming the Woman of His Dreams is a thoughtful look at the wonderful, unique, and God-ordained role a woman has in her husband's life. Sharon Jaynes offers seven key qualities every wife should strive for.

THE POWER OF A PRAYING® WIFE
Stormie Omartian

Stormie Omartian shares how you can develop a deeper relationship with your husband by praying for him. Packed with practical advice on praying for specific areas, including decision-making, fears, spiritual strength, and sexuality, this book will help you discover the fulfilling marriage God intended.

HARVEST HOUSE
PUBLISHERS